CW01499563

Contents

RECIPES

Preface

For years I had been searching for something that I truly wanted to do with my life.

Alex, an ex-boss and old friend, so believed in my ability, he invited me to travel from our home in New Zealand and stay with his family for a week in LA to investigate a women's gym franchise he wanted me to manage on his behalf. I could see how it would work but it needed a 24-hour commitment. My husband, Steve, and I still had young children then and I couldn't give my all to both. The kids came first.

Some years later nothing was satisfying me work-wise and I wanted to do something that I felt passionate about. For me this usually involved people. When going out or travelling with friends, they would roll their eyes as 'Annemarie's found another new best friend'. Somehow I would end up chatting with people wherever we were. I loved hearing their stories of where they came from and how they lived their lives.

Because of this and the amount of travel Steve and I had done, I decided to establish my own private tourism business. The concept was to meet clients at the airport or off the cruise ships, deliver them to their hotel and later transport them around the Greater Auckland area of New Zealand. I would offer personalised shopping and take them to galleries and points of interest and to meet artisans of food, art and culture. My website was up and running and the brochures printed. I'd approached several major hotels to see if they would offer me as part of their concierge service. They liked the idea but I needed a very nice car as my clientele would be mainly high-net-worth individuals.

Back then we didn't have the funds to buy an appropriate vehicle or to advertise in the US and UK travel magazines. Also, when I took a cold, hard look at myself I discovered I didn't have the self-belief or the confidence needed to see it all through. In trepidation I took Steve out for a walk, sat him down on a park bench and apologised for the money I'd spent so far. I told him I didn't think I could see my plan through. That was a hard thing for me to do. He was very understanding and didn't actually care about the money. The only comment he made was 'at least you had a go'.

Feeling so restless and loving all our travels, I was online constantly looking at overseas jobs. Quite by chance one Sunday afternoon while idly scrolling through a couple of sites, my dream job in France filled the screen. I couldn't believe it. Let me tell you how it all unfolded…

My story is dedicated to Andy Wilson. Andy was my friend for 30 years and an inspiration to all. He was a loving husband and father, kind and caring and a good friend to many people around the world. An enormously clever, generous, positive and forward-thinking man, Andy encouraged me to turn our experience into a book.

Andy, this is for you.
Rest in peace, my friend.
Annemarie

1

Chasing the Dream

My hands were shaking as I punched in the phone number. It was ringing. 'Brrr, brrr. Brrr, brrr.'

'Come on, come on, pick up, Ginny,' I murmured to myself, pacing up and down the kitchen.

'Hi, Annemarie, how are you?' Ginny, my girlfriend, asked as she finally answered my call.

'Ginny, listen, listen,' I said breathlessly.

'You OK, Annemarie? What's up?' she asked.

'You're not going to believe this, Gin. Steve and I are moving to France! We've just been offered a job in Southwest France. I'm beyond excited. We're to manage a private country home for a London-based couple and host them, their friends and any paying guests who may wish to rent the house.'

'Oh my god, Annemarie! That's incredible. How fantastic for you. Oh I'll miss you. No, scratch that. I'm coming to visit you! Oh this is so exciting.'

We talked for ages, mashing through all the preparations Steve and I needed to make and how it was all going to work. Half an hour later, we said our goodbyes.

My travels to Europe with Steve had always included a stay somewhere in France. After loving every French visit, I'd become obsessed with finding a way to spend more time there, to get to know the people and enjoy the food and culture. A while ago I'd discovered online jobs via the The Lady website and also Gumtree, which advertises absolutely everything. In our case, it was the perfect job. It was one late-January afternoon in 2014 that my dream had leapt off the screen. The advert read:

We are seeking the right couple to manage and take care of a beautiful 15th-century farmhouse, Mas de Lavande, in Southwest France. It is a private home as well as a holiday rental. Your skillset will include excellent management, gardening, cooking and housekeeping abilities. You must have a clean driver's licence. The successful applicants will be well-presented and hard-working. Experience in managing and maintaining a large home and property is essential. You will be able to provide exceptional hospitality, to both family and guests. A love of animals is essential. You will also be able to manage and undertake the expansion of the rental side of the property, maintaining an excellent booking system. French language is an asset but not a necessity.

My treasured memories of France came flooding back: sunflower, rapeseed and lavender fields; beautiful wine and food markets; exploring pretty villages and driving down narrow country roads under sunny, blue skies.

I'd grabbed Steve by the arm, dragged him into our home office, waggled my fingers at my laptop screen and stuttered, 'This is us! This is us! We're perfect for this job.'

Both of us had plenty of business and management experience. Steve had been in the construction industry and I was a personal assistant in my earlier working life, before children. Later, when our children were young, my working roles had encompassed office manager and part-time receptionist duties. These occupations required us to build relationships and to get on well with people. Also Steve loved creating order in our garden and nothing gave me more pleasure than cooking and welcoming friends and family to our home. I'd project-managed and interior-designed the renovation of our large home. These skills ticked off 99% of the prerequisites on the list.

Steve looked at me, shrugged his shoulders and calmly said, 'Well, my contract finishes in the middle of February. There's no harm in applying.' Before Steve had even left the room, my fingers were flying across the keyboard, sending off our application.

We'd often talked about how we could make our dream of living and working in France happen. We'd even purchased a book on the topic. The biggest hurdle we'd faced was that neither of us had the right to a passport from a European country. Or did we? When Steve re-checked the eligibility criteria, he realised he *could* get that vital document. His mother had been born in Scotland which gave him all the eligibility he needed. The previous November, Steve had completed the passport application in the hope that we could secure work overseas, sent it all off and then went for his face-to-face interview. *Voilà*, a month later his UK passport had arrived.

Steve had a few days' work in Wellington so I decided to go, too. It would be a good time to catch up with my family. I tried to put the whole French thing to the back of my mind but it all kept rolling around in my head. I was having trouble sleeping. Two days later I thought my heart was going to jump out of my chest when I opened my email and found a very positive reply from the London agent, with a detailed job description attached:

House Maintenance

- security of house and grounds
- door, shutter, window maintenance
- lighting and bulbs
- outdoor furniture maintenance

- gutter cleaning
- rodent control

Housekeeping

- housework, polishing floors, cleaning windows
- kitchen cleaning and organisation
- laundry—all linen
- bed-making
- stocking cleaning materials
- organising boiler service, chimney sweeping
- ordering fuels—oil and gas
- rubbish removal
- fireplace cleaning, filling log baskets
- grocery shopping
- treating of sinks, showers, drains

Cooking

- cooking dinner up to three times per week when owners in residence
- preparing breakfast/lunch and/or dinner when guests present
- using produce from the kitchen garden and orchard
- organising informal dinner parties

Grounds

- grass cutting
- weeding, edging
- fertilising
- cutting hedges
- watering
- tractor, lawnmower and equipment maintenance
- replacing plants as necessary

- cars—cleaning, maintenance, servicing
- septic tank control
- fencing maintenance
- patio cleaning
- irrigation system controls

Pool

- annual set-up and close-down
- weekly maintenance
- control of pH levels
- setting up/storing furniture

General

- investigating options for leisure activities in the area
- developing future business for holiday lettings
- developing a handbook for guest use
- meeting and greeting guests with warmth and ensuring the best guest experience
- airport collection/drop-off
- weekly reports
- flexibility

Animals

- taking care of cats, dogs and chickens
- vet as necessary

My god! What a list. The agency advertising the position was a Richmond-based lifestyle company in London. It looked after an individual's every need and want—in this instance, finding estate managers for a property in France. The agent we were dealing with was Sarah. She asked us to take a good look at the job description and everything it entailed. If we felt we met all the criteria and would like to go to the next step, we were to get back in touch. Of course we wanted to go to the next step! The only thing listed that we hadn't done before was looking after chickens. How hard could that be?

I certainly wasn't going to let a little thing such as having a conversation in French hold me back. Just for once I'd let Steve do all the talking. He'd taken French for five years at secondary school and one year at university. During the previous two years, Steve had also attended *Alliance Française* classes. My French language was limited to my third-form lessons at secondary school.

After several Skype interviews with a rather imperious Sarah, a brief one with Tristan (the co-owner of Mas de Lavande and owner of an art gallery in Richmond), references were gathered and emails flew back and forth. Waiting to hear back was nerve-wracking but two weeks later, we received the sorry news that we were unsuccessful. Tristan wanted a couple there as soon as possible. The problem was that we were on the other side of the world, with an entire household and life to pack up before we could even think about leaving the country.

I was so upset. But why would they even consider two people in their early 50s who lived 12,000 miles away? I wasn't being very realistic. Steve asked Sarah to get back to us if the successful couple didn't work out. I felt so dejected and found it very difficult to get back into the groove of everyday life. I'd been daydreaming about sunflower fields, lush, green pastures and a beautiful, old French home.

Several weeks later it was my birthday. Steve gave me a card in which he'd written: I hope all your dreams come true for you. He knew how disappointed I'd been and was trying to be kind. As I flipped open my iPad and checked our emails, my heart thumped all over again.

'Yes, yes, yes!' I yelled, punching the air in our home office. I ran down the hallway, calling. 'Steve, Steve, where are you?'

'Here, in the front garden,' he called. 'What's all the yelling about? I could hear you out here,' he said as I reached the doorstep.

'Sarah, the agent, has emailed us. The couple Tristan and Richard, his partner, had chosen have taken a job elsewhere. They're now offering the job to us!' I said breathlessly. 'Sarah has sent a link to one of the rental websites to check out the photos. Come in and we can take a look together and then word our response,' I suggested, excited beyond words.

'Hold your horses!' Steve drawled. 'Let me just finish digging here and I'll be in in 20 minutes. There's no panic.'

Not for him there wasn't. There always was for me—Mrs Impatient! Half an hour later, Steve came in, drying his hands as he wandered up to the office, and stood behind me. Sitting in my chair, I already had the website up and was working my way through the photos.

'Look at the house, Steve. It's gorgeous. I love the pale mossy-green shutters. And the creamy-coloured stone. It looks to have great proportions, too. You know, that rectangular shape. It's so classically French,' I gushed. Bathed in sunshine, it looked idyllic and I couldn't wait to get there.

'It sure looks pretty nice. Bring up some of the interior ones. Let's have a look at the inside,' he said, leaning in for a closer inspection.

We spent another half hour checking out the rest of the photos then worded our response to Sarah. I hit 'enter' and the email was gone, accepting the position of estate managers and a new life in France.

There was still a lot for us to talk about and organise. Ten days later all the details were finalised and we were about to embark on moving our lives to the other side of the world and start living the dream.

2

Preparing to Leave

I couldn't see how we were ever going to leave New Zealand. It was mind-boggling what we needed to arrange: insurances, storage facilities, renting out the house, selling the cars. The list seemed to get longer, not shorter. Then there was the decluttering while we were packing up. Our home office and garage contained mountains of paperwork that we didn't need to refer to again. My husband begged to differ. He's a bit of a hoarder. Our tempers were getting frayed with all that we had to do.

'Honestly, Steve, this is ridiculous! We don't need these old receipts and invoices. You have to shred them. I'm not paying for them to go into storage; it's just a waste of money,' I snapped at him. 'And how many copies of our passports and licences do we really need? Six of each is over the top.'

'Well, that's your opinion. I'm keeping them,' he said dismissively.

We were having some rather heated 'discussions' about what was *necessary* to keep and what wasn't.

Our furniture was going into storage, with some pieces spread amongst the family. We'd packed hundreds of books into boxes for storage and given just as many away. Time was quickly ticking by. We raced to list saleable items on Trade Me (New Zealand's version of eBay). Everything we didn't need in our last few weeks was already packed, ready for storage. Steve decided a refresher in French would be useful so booked himself in for private lessons with a local French teacher.

Our tickets were all booked. So that we could meet Tristan, Richard and Sarah, we would be overnighting in London and our flight to Toulouse would be the day after. We were looking forward to meeting the owners. Tristan had the art gallery and Richard was a partner in a busy City law firm. Both of them were Londoners and they'd met at the launch party for an artist friend of Tristan's. Sarah wasn't giving away much but did let slip it was love at first sight and they'd been together for over 30 years. We'd spoken via Skype several times with Sarah but we'd only had one fleeting conversation with Tristan. Richard was yet to materialise. The face-to-face get-together with everyone would give us all a better feel for what each of us was like.

I was getting antsy as Sarah had been a bit slap-dash in communicating with us since we'd accepted the job and often didn't call at pre-arranged times. There would always be an apology (and an excuse) but it was rather frustrating as the time zones were over 12 hours apart. Often we sat up late at night, waiting for the Skype call to come through or for answers to our emails to arrive, usually in vain and when a reply did come, a lot of questions were still unanswered. During our last week in New Zealand, I took the bull by the horns and drafted up a terms of employment letter. We hadn't received anything from Sarah and we wanted there to be something in writing between us. It came back signed by Tristan, but only the day before we left. I was starting to question how efficient Sarah was. We found out that she was a struggling artist who had begun painting in her late 30s. Tristan had taken her under his wing, trying to help her out. Sarah only worked part-time for the lifestyle agency to earn extra cash.

Our social diary was filled with last-minute dinners and

lunches with family and friends. We also planned an 'open home' so people could drop in for a drink to say bon voyage. Who knew how long we would be away? I was dreading the farewell part as we had such a fantastic network of good friends whom we saw often. I had to push these thoughts to the back of my mind and not dwell on them.

Our bon voyage drinks were great fun and led seamlessly on to a buffet dinner of cooked ham on the bone, roast vegetable salad, green salad and bread rolls. Dessert was roasted nectarines, peaches and apricots with Greek yoghurt and my homemade lemon ice cream. Everyone was able to spill out onto the deck to enjoy the warm summer evening. While putting together a platter of food at the kitchen bench, I looked up at our friends and family gathered in the living room and on the deck. I had a moment of 'oh God, how am I going to cope without everyone in my daily life?' *That* was going to be the hardest thing for me to deal with. We didn't know anyone in France. We had limited French language skills and we would be solely relying on each other for company, 24 hours a day. It didn't help that I'm a chatterbox and Steve isn't. He would very quickly need to get used to me using up my female quota of 10,000 words a day on him. That, or don some sort of ear protection.

Our leaving seemed long and protracted and saying goodbye was hard. Some friends thought us quite mad for upping sticks and flying halfway around the world to work. Our lives were changing from a corporate, city one to country living and animal husbandry.

The worst part of going would be leaving our youngest son. It made me feel ill every time I thought about it. Our eldest son was, thankfully, happy working and living in Australia. I knew the youngest was an adult and leading his own life but he hadn't yet left home and the thought that I wanted to see him settled into a flat before we left was uppermost in my mind. You never stop being a mother, no matter how old they are. Would he eat well? Not drink too much? What about his university work? I had to remember I couldn't control everything…as much as Steve often said I would have liked to.

The countdown was on and there were only five days to go before we were due to leave. Our house was a bombsite. Everywhere we turned, stuff was piled up, waiting to be wrapped and packed. I'd laid our clothes out on the bed; I just needed to put them into suitcases. As I looked at the pile, I could tell we would be paying for excess luggage. *Should I take my little black dress? Will I need my high heels out in the country? No. Hang on a minute. I might just go somewhere posh at some stage.* I slipped them into my suitcase. We would be gone a minimum of one year so it was hard to know what to take, what to leave and for some of us (read—husband) what to throw out.

On our last day at home, the packers arrived early to make a start on the kitchen, glassware and paintings. That night we moved in with our friends, Ann and Kevin. Our youngest son came and joined us for dinner for the last time before we headed off. He'd found a good flat and was well settled in, which made me feel a little better. He loved his part-time job so life was looking good for him. And his university work? I did hope he loved that just as much.

At long last it was time for us to leave. We arrived at Auckland Airport after a rather stressful last few hours for me, waiting for Steve to finish. My packed bags and I were ready at the door but Steve had decided he wanted to do some last-minute work back at our home. He was cutting it very fine to get to the airport. Steve wears a corporate-world moniker of 'the late Mr Rawson'.

I was so glad we'd already said goodbye to our youngest son and he wouldn't be at the airport. I would have hung onto him, fighting back tears and issuing last-minute instructions on how he was to live his life. I had no idea when we would see him again.

3

London Stopover

Our direct flight to Heathrow was uneventful but exhausting. Sarah was there, waiting to collect us. On Skype calls you only see a person sitting down so I was taken aback at how tall Sarah was. She must have been close to six foot, was very slim and nicely dressed—wearing a white shirt and navy skirt and jacket—until I spotted her shoes. They were very tatty and scuffed, tan ankle boots and definitely didn't go with the semi-formal work attire. I don't know why but those awful boots swam into my vision every time we later spoke to her on Skype or by phone.

Sarah dropped us outside the B&B in Richmond. We checked in and got ourselves up to our room. I was desperate for a shower and a change of clothes.

'What did you make of Sarah?' Steve asked me, rifling through his suitcase for underwear and a fresh shirt. His jeans were fairly new and would have to do to wear to dinner. They didn't look too creased up.

'She was a bit abrupt, didn't you think? Wasn't very welcoming. She certainly didn't offer a lot of conversation,' I said, shaking out a dress and placing it on a hanger in the wardrobe. 'And what about those boots! Ugh.'

'No, she didn't say much but she seemed pleasant enough. Remember she didn't offer a lot when we were on Skype? Always distracted and shuffling papers. Sarah always had other places to be. She was often clipped in her conversations then,' Steve reminded me, heading for the bathroom.

'True. Maybe she's just rather conservative?' I suggested. 'I hope she thaws out a bit and lets us get to know her. We've got to work with her. Hey! Let me have first shower. I've got to put make-up on and will take longer than you,' I said, elbowing Steve out of the bathroom doorway.

'Hurry up or I'll fall asleep on this bed before you're done,' he teased, pretending to lie down.

That afternoon we visited Tristan's art gallery and workshop in Richmond. He wasn't there but we went into the back office and worked through the job description and programme for the summer with Sarah. It was only then that we received a complete list of what needed doing as soon as we arrived in France.

'Oh, yes, Tristan wants you to do a full household inventory when you get there. It hasn't been done for a couple of years. You'll need to count, photograph and document every piece of linen, knife, fork and spoon. Also all glassware, pots, pans and cookware,' Sarah advised.

'Oh, OK. Yes, we can do that, no problem,' I said. *Heavens*, I thought. *That'll take days to do.*

We were so ignorant of the actual work involved but Steve and I would need to hit the ground running. There were already several bookings for Mas de Lavande over the summer. A large art club group from Cornwall were booked for a week as well as two separate artists' workshop weeks. We also learnt that Tristan opened the house once a year at the end of summer for an art auction. This brought in so many of the English and French from Toulouse to Albi and was a lucrative cash injection.

Steve and I were very comfortable at dinner that night at

Tristan and Richard's home on Richmond Hill. Richmond is an area where lots of actors, artists and musicians have made their homes in some of the most beautiful 18th- and 19th-century buildings. It's a stunning London suburb.

The housekeeper warmly greeted us at the door. Tristan and Richard's taste in décor was an eclectic mix of styles: English, Italian and French. My favourite flowers, phalaenopsis orchids, were everywhere throughout the house. Some were planted in antique Italian urns and others in old, blue and white china tureens. These tureens sat on beautiful, glossy, mahogany, semi-circular tables in the hall, adding a little luxury to the entranceway. It was all so very English and looked like something out of *House and Garden* magazine. I loved it. The walls were covered with paintings and objets d'art. I guessed these were regularly rotated through the gallery.

This was going to be our opportunity to get to know Tristan and Richard a little. Sarah joined us for dinner and seemed more relaxed and pleasant. We congregated in the kitchen to have drinks while dinner was finishing off in the oven. It wasn't a huge kitchen, but very workable with a painted butcher's block for a centre island. Appliances sat to one side on the bench, which had a white-tiled splashback. Everything was decorated in neutral colours and gave a blank canvas for yet more colourful art.

Dinner was simple but delicious: sliced, cold roast beef with horseradish, new potatoes, asparagus and a tossed salad with a creamy balsamic dressing. Dessert was fresh berries, cream and lemon tart. All the food was easy to prepare, with no fuss. This was to set the scene for how they liked to eat at the house in France. No fancy sauces or haute cuisine. I was very happy as that's exactly how I liked to cook and eat, too.

'So, Annemarie, Steve, I do apologise that Richard isn't here to meet you. He's at a client dinner he couldn't excuse himself from, unfortunately. I guess you'll meet him at some stage, down at the farmhouse,' Tristan said, standing up to refill our glasses. 'Richard's an extremely busy man in his City practice and doesn't want to deal with anything to do with the French property. He's very happy for Sarah and me to handle everything so you'll be communicating with the two of us.'

Tristan appeared pleasant enough, quite chatty, although he never actually made eye contact. I thought at the time that perhaps he was a bit shy. He looked to be early 60s, quite tall, slim and dressed in a beautiful, floral, cotton shirt, chinos and navy suede loafers. His straight, steely-grey hair was immaculately cut. The conversation at the dinner table centred on their French home.

'The farmhouse is where we like to go to chill out. Our lives are rather hectic here and it's one place we can be informal and relax. However, we have high standards and expect the house to be well-kept,' Tristan emphasised. 'There will be various friends of ours going to stay there over the summer when we aren't there. They're not difficult people and they know they're to look after themselves in terms of cooking but please make them welcome,' he added. 'Sarah will let you know when as soon as they book dates with her.'

'Of course, Tristan. Don't worry, we'll make them very welcome and help if they need it,' I reassured him.

Steve nodded beside me, saying, 'Not a problem at all.'

Mid-morning the next day, Sarah handed us our working contract which hadn't been ready before we left Auckland. Steve and I had asked for it several times but with everything going on at home it never got followed up. A bit like the expanded job description, it was a last-minute thing. We were already running late for our flight to Toulouse so the contract had to be quickly signed, photocopied and a copy stashed into our hand luggage. There was no time to read it. We'd have to do that at a later date. Not good. I was so keen to get to France and to get a good deal on flights, and rather than relying on last-minute availability, I'd gone ahead and booked flights early. This was before we'd received either the job contract or the expanded job description.

Hindsight is a fine thing. I was too trusting. I should have insisted on having all the paperwork before booking flights. A big mistake and, unfortunately, it was all too late. We'd already made the commitment. We'd rented out our house, stored the furniture and we were halfway around the world.

4

A la Maison

After we'd touched down at Toulouse Airport, we waited and waited for Steve's golf clubs to appear at the baggage claim. No such luck. We made arrangements to have them delivered to the house once they turned up. Finally we emerged. Waiting for us with a beaming, welcoming smile was Doug. He was married to Siobhan, a woman he'd met in Wellington, New Zealand, the city Steve and I grew up in. We smiled at the fact they'd met in our home town. They'd been living in France for eight years. Doug and Siobhan were English and were also employed by the lifestyle company in Richmond, overseeing several properties in the area.

The motorway journey to our new home was a complex system of roads. They continuously intersected and whizzed past until we got out into the countryside. There was no way I could have found my way back to the airport. And the speed of all the traffic! Oh my goodness; it was way too fast for me.

It was early evening when we arrived at the farmhouse, near Brens. A pinky dusk streaked the skyline and the air had cleared after the thunderstorm that had greeted us when we landed. As we turned into the lavender-lined drive, I couldn't help but gasp at seeing the main house, captured in the golden halo of the car headlights. It was exactly as I'd pictured it: a three-storeyed, cream-coloured stone farmhouse, with old wooden shutters painted in a light moss-green colour. A bare wisteria vine framed the double-fronted door and windows. As we stepped out of the car, there was a definite chill in the air. I pulled my jacket tightly around me and we stood for a moment in the fading light, absorbing the lush, green, rolling landscape and the silhouetted orchard of bare fruit trees. A large, rickety, three-sided barn sat on the other side of the drive. We could make out a rusty, green tractor and what looked to be a stack of old furniture and an awful lot of junk piled up. Tucked behind the barn, there appeared to be a half-finished building. Tomorrow would be the time to explore and check the whole property out.

'Until your cottage is ready,' Sarah had told us, 'you'll be staying in the renovated *pigeonnier*—a house for pigeons.'

'Pigeons?' I asked.

'Yes, *pigeonniers* have been in use for centuries. They either stood alone or were built as part of the main house.'

'Do many houses have them?' I quizzed her.

'They're very common in the southwest of France. Pigeons were kept for their eggs and flesh and the dung was used to fertilise the home grapevines.'

Pulling our suitcases behind us, we trundled down the path. As we approached the *pigeonnier*, it was heartening to see the golden glow of lamplights shining through the little front door window panes. The warmth from the radiators enveloped us as we entered the tiny foyer. Spring flowers, sitting in a pretty blue bowl on the hall table, gave off a floral and sweet fragrance.

'Oh, by the way, the flowers are a welcome gift from Tristan and Richard,' grunted Doug as he lumbered through the door with the extra suitcase. 'And Siobhan has been to the supermarket, knowing you were held up. Just so you'd have some food for dinner as well as a little something for breakfast. You'll find the bed is made up and fresh towels are in the bathroom already.'

Siobhan had left everything on the kitchen table, along with two bottles of local wine. How nice. We needn't worry about anything until the morning. It had all been done for us.

'Thank you so much, Doug. You've been so helpful. Please say many thanks to Siobhan for everything. Hopefully we'll catch up with you both soon?' I suggested.

'Oh yes. Siobhan will be popping in late afternoon tomorrow to say hello. Here are our phone numbers if you need anything,' Doug said, handing me a slip of paper. 'I'll be off then. Cheerio.'

The door had only just closed behind Doug when Steve announced, 'I'm starving.' I managed to get the gas cooker working and rustled up a steak with a few vegetables. Steve found plates, cutlery and glassware on the curtained, under-bench shelves. He pulled the cork from one of the wine bottles with a satisfying pop and poured the blush-pink liquid into a couple of glasses. Now that we'd finally arrived, I flopped into the nearest chair and we raised our glasses, toasting our new French life with a delicious floral rosé.

With dinner and dishes done, we had a good explore of the *pigeonnier*. It was so pretty and very charming. The main bedroom furnishings were sewn in an old, French, pinky-red *toile de Jouy* fabric, including the drapes. It looked perfect for the age of Mas de Lavande and so very French chic. Our room was large and furnished with a panelled, pale oak armoire, a big, comfy armchair and two fabric-covered, glass-topped side tables. Tall reading lamps sat on each of the bedside tables. The en-suite bathroom, although rudimentary and rustic, was fine. The vanity top was fully tiled, with the hand basin set on it. A pretty, checked-pink curtain covered the single shelf beneath it. The shower stall was also tiled but the grout had seen better days. It looked as though it would come up alright with a decent scrub. The tiled floor throughout the bedroom and bathroom was old, burnished-red terracotta.

Across the flagstone-floored hallway was a second bedroom

with two single, iron-framed beds. The room was simply decorated like ours and very sweet. The bed covers were embossed white cotton duvets. Blue *toile de Jouy* quilts sat neatly folded on the end of each one and the same pretty blue fabric had been made into curtains and light shades on the wooden bedside lamps. A bleached-oak set of drawers, with round, black, iron pull-ring handles, sat against one wall. Back in the hallway, a narrow, painted staircase led up to a smaller bedroom. This room had a high double bed and an antique wooden desk and a chair. A squishy, old armchair was tucked into the corner. Above the bed was a tiny, four-paned window, recessed into the wall. This filled the original opening where the pigeons would have come in and out.

It was time for bed. Both of us were yawning like crazy. That first night it was wonderful to crawl into that huge bed and pull the thick, downy duvet up under our chins. I think we were asleep before our heads hit the pillows.

After breakfast the following morning, it was time to explore the main house. The early morning, grey mist was starting to lift and fine-fingered rays of sunshine were slicing through the filmy sky. It was a beautiful farmhouse with great bones. I couldn't wait until the summer when the soft purple blooms of the wisteria would be out. These would be beautiful and would set off the cream stone to perfection. The fragrance would be intense. As time went on, we discovered many similar farmhouses as the style was typical of the area.

Entering the house for the first time, I stopped in my tracks. The interior was nothing like the charming and inviting house it appeared on the outside. There was a damp, musty smell. The first bedroom we entered revealed the covers on the bed carelessly thrown back. It looked like someone had got up that very morning and walked out. The stone floor was thick with layers of dust and dead flies. Soiled towels lay on the en-suite floor. Dried-up soap-ends and filthy scum were stuck to the hand basin and the toilet was thick with green mould. It hadn't been cleaned in months. I started to retch. What was going on here?

Walking into the kitchen was soul-destroying. My heart was hammering, for all the wrong reasons. The rough-cast stone floor was ingrained with a century of dirt and grime. The top of the wooden centre island was crisscrossed with mould-filled, black lines. Food had been cut on it and no one had bothered to use a board or to wipe it down. That would need hauling outside and boiling, soapy water poured over it, then I'd have to attack it with a scrubbing brush if I was to get it anywhere near hygienic. The gas hobs were encrusted in thick, hard mould, the result of spilt-over food. A door was hanging off one of the ovens. The knives looked cheap and blunt. A mixture of old, battered pots and pans hung from nails in the beams. Cracked casseroles and chipped plates sat on dirty shelves. On every surface in the kitchen was a layer of what looked like fine salt. It wasn't. We discovered it was from the crumbling ceiling above which had never been coated or sealed.

'I feel sick,' I groaned to Steve. 'This is where I'll spend most of my time during our tenure here. How on earth am I going to prepare food properly in this kitchen? How long will it take to get this place into any fit state to work in?'

Steve didn't need to reply. The look on his face said it all.

The rest of the house was in reasonable but very shabby shape. Every room needed a thorough clean from top to bottom. The grime and damp were palpable to me. With so many rooms needing detailed attention, it was going to take weeks to get it fresh and sparkling. I felt completely overwhelmed with what needed doing. I slumped into the nearest chair, holding my head in my hands and fighting back the tears. My dreams of a beautiful, old, French farmhouse with classic interiors were ridiculous. The house certainly didn't look anything like the online images or photos we'd been sent.

The top storey used to be the attic but during a renovation it was converted into three bedrooms. The rooms had rooflines sloped so low, the tiny, four-paned windows only came up to our knees. On the other side of the landing was a bathroom with a huge, old, claw-footed bath. It also housed a filthy toilet and a single pedestal basin, standing on a much-scuffed, painted floor.

'What the hell have we done, Steve? It's going to take weeks to get it fresh and habitable. Then there's the inventory on top of all this,' I wailed.

'I know. It's pretty bad. C'mon. Let's go and see what state the cottage is in,' he suggested.

Once outside and after taking some deep breaths, we walked back down the path. The cottage was going to be our new home. It was renovated about 20 years ago and was more modern than the other buildings. It only had three rooms: a bathroom, a bedroom and a sitting/dining room/kitchenette. It was small and at first glance through the French doors, liveable. Once inside, though, it was a different story. We found half-empty bottles, dirty glasses, mouldy food in containers and newspapers strewn over the table. Odd items of clothing hung in the wardrobe and the bathroom cabinet was full of toiletries. Did these belong to the last guardians? Why would they leave it that way? We discovered why a month or so later.

The sofa was very shabby with a dirty, old bedspread thrown over it as a cover. Four mismatched, partly broken chairs were set around the wooden table.

'There's no way we can move in here with it looking like it does, Steve. It's filthy! Everything needs a thorough clean and scrub down,' I said turning and taking in my surroundings. 'We're going to have to put all the linen, cushion covers, the lot, through the washing machine. And what on earth is that awful smell?' I wrinkled my nose at him.

'It's pretty bad, alright,' Steve agreed, grimacing. 'Remember

Sarah told us Tristan was going to update the cottage? We're supposed to make a list of what we need and send it through to her,' Steve reminded me.

'Thank heavens for that. We can't live in it in any sense of comfort as it is.'

Before going into the main house, we'd let the chickens out of the coop to fossick[1] around in the yard. Getting them back in that evening was very easy. All I had to do was make chook noises and they followed me. They must have recognised an 'old boiler'.

Behind the coop was the large kitchen garden, completely bare except for a small patch of leeks, a large and expired Jerusalem artichoke plant and some weeds. The earth looked rock-hard after a freezing cold winter. All the lawns around the property were knee-high. The swimming pool was in a major state of disrepair, filled a foot deep with filthy rainwater and debris. These areas too, would take weeks to get ready for the family and guests. Mas de Lavande had been neglected for months and months. With a combination of jet lag, tiredness and shock at the state of the property, I felt very low. The amount of work required to get the house habitable was overwhelming. All this, before I could even think about cooking. Tears weren't far away.

Steve was keen to shake me out of my despair.

'Right, Annemarie, you need a change of scenery,' he cajoled, putting his arm around me. 'We need to get some groceries in so let's go find what's open and have a look around.'

We took ourselves off in the battered and beaten-up Citroën provided for our use to check out the area. We drove on to Albi to get some groceries as nothing was open in our village. After getting lost several times, we finally found our way back, in time to meet Siobhan, Doug's wife.

'Hiya,' she called, getting out of the car and smiling broadly at us. 'How are you getting on? Found everything you need?'

What a friendly welcome. I put the kettle on and we sat over a comforting cuppa and talked for ages. It was as if we'd known each other forever.

As she stood up to leave, she said, 'I don't know if you're interested but every year there's a quiz night held in the village. You would be very welcome to come with us. Everyone takes a bottle of wine and joins in. All the kids come along, too.'

We leapt at the chance to go out and be part of an activity with the locals. 'Thank you, Siobhan. We'd love that,' I beamed.

'Right, well put it in your hectic social calendar,' she grinned. 'You can come and have supper with us before we go. Nothing fancy mind. A BBQ most likely and we'll be having some family staying with us then, too, so it should be a fun night.'

We were so looking forward to it, to try and begin an everyday life and become part of the community. Both Siobhan and Doug seemed very easy to get on with. We hoped to see more of them.

In an attempt to cope with the jet lag, Steve and I rugged up[2] after dinner and went walking. It was early spring and was still quite cold. I had three layers on, plus a woollen hat. There were no footpaths so we were on the road and needed to listen out for any cars approaching. Only two passed us the whole hour we were out. We came across fields of sunflowers, just starting to push their way up through the soil. We couldn't identify them as sunflowers that night but there was no mistaking what they were a few months later. It was very rural where we were living. A few homes dotted the immediate landscape, one being a B&B that we would eventually check out. There would be more staff than beds available during the summer peak so we would need to house them somewhere.

As we walked we could hear an incredible racket coming from further along the road and the closer we got, the louder it became. We thought it was machinery. Instead we discovered hundreds of frogs in a high-sided, stagnant pond making the strangest noise. We could hardly hear each other talk, it was so loud. We guessed it was mating season.

Back at the *pigeonnier,* we hauled off our hats and jackets and kicked off our shoes. Both of us had great difficulty stifling yawns and keeping our eyes open. Soon we were tucked up in bed, so cosy under the duvet and fast asleep before it was even dark. Bliss.

During the following days, panic attacks gripped me. It was difficult to stem my constant tide of tears and to untie the knots in my stomach. I couldn't eat as I felt constantly sick.

We'd delved further into the house, the barn, the half-finished outbuilding and the storage areas. I felt so distressed by what we'd taken on. Mas de Lavande was nothing like the photos nor my romantic imaginings of everything being ready for us to walk in and to start work. I felt so foolish. The reality was starting to hit home. We were going to be skivvies for at least a month, trying to get the place up to scratch. Is that why the first chosen couple decided not to take the job? Had they been to check it out and seen just how much work it would take *before* any guests arrived? Probably.

On the first couple of nights, while Steve slept, I was in the kitchen, whispering and crying into my laptop.

I was on Skype with Barb, a good friend back in New Zealand.

'God, Barb, I think I've made a terrible mistake,' I sobbed. 'Maybe it's a combination of jet lag, tiredness and being away from home and all of you.'

'Listen to me; you will most definitely be jet-lagged and exhausted. You had so much to get done before you left. You're run ragged before you even begin there, you two were so busy,' Barb said firmly. 'It's very early days. You haven't even been there a week! Give yourself time,' she said realistically.

'I know. It's just all so overwhelming at the moment. Finding the house so filthy has been such a shock. I can't even begin to think about cooking for a crowd, let alone dinner for just one night. My head feels all woolly and I can't focus. I've got to get to grips with the supermarket as well, working out the French equivalent of what I use at home,' I wailed. 'What the hell have I done, Barb?'

'You can do this, Annemarie. We know what you're made of,' Barb encouraged. 'I'm going to go now and I want you to get into bed, snuggle up to Steve and try to calm your mind. You need to sleep. Let's talk in a couple of days. I know you'll be feeling a lot better then. Just give yourself time. Hear me? Give yourself time.'

I did as she suggested and crawled into bed, welcoming the warmth of Steve already there. He was so positive and strong. I had to absorb this myself and get moving. All I wanted to do was stay under the duvet and hide. I hoped and prayed that my outlook would become more positive after a few nights of sleep.

---

1. To search for.
2. Dressed warmly.

5

Country Life

I wish you could have seen Steve. He was in his element, in his New Zealand stubbies[1], T-shirt and cap on the ride-on lawnmower. Gabriel, the gardener, had been in and given Steve chapter and verse on the property and the intricacies of the ride-on. He pointed out to him where all the old stumps and stones were throughout the lawned area and told him he needed to avoid these at all costs or they would wreck the mower.

There was Steve, careering round the vast back lawn, trying to get the grass length under control. I sat outside at the little café table enjoying a glass of rosé, watching him. It was a little after 6 p.m. and still so warm. A warning, I thought, of how hot it was going to get during the summer months. There was a frog stuck in the swimming pool in about an inch of scummy water. It was making very loud ribbit-ribbit noises to great effect in that echo chamber. As soon as I went near, it dived under but we couldn't get it out, even with the pool skimming net.

The feral cats were starting to get a little braver and kept peeking in our front door, as did the chickens. After observing these feathered creatures and their antics, I'd named them: Maggie Hatcher, Elle Macpherson, Hilda Ogden[2] and Adele.

Maggie Hatcher was the obvious matriarch and so bossy. She would strut about, corralling and clucking at the others if they strayed from the brood. Elle Macpherson had long legs and beautiful plumage and was forever grooming herself. Poor Hilda Ogden was an old hen, very scruffy and always scratching in the dirt, looking for that elusive little gem of something, and had such a shrill cackle. As for Adele, well she was gorgeous: golden feathers, full-breasted and she could belt out the loudest continuous squawks.

Our first week was hectic. We got down to work straight away and I laundered continually. We stripped the linen from every bed in the house, not knowing when the beds were last slept in. In each room Steve moved mattresses into the sunlight to air. We latched the shutters open and when the sun was out, I opened the windows and doors to allow fresh air to circulate through the house. Every toilet and bathroom had been scrubbed. The filthy butcher's block was now fit to be used after I'd attacked it with boiling water, soap and scrubbing brush. We discovered workmen had been living in the house. Once their project was finished, they'd walked out of the door, not giving a damn about the mess they left.

Late one afternoon we walked up to explore our little village. Unfortunately everything was shut as it was yet another public holiday. En-route we passed a family playing boules in their front yard. Their rooster was cock-a-doodle-dooing at full throttle while hens clucked and scratched in the yard dirt. We called out a friendly *bonjour* and they responded, but with obvious curiosity. We were noticeably new to the area.

In the village two old gentlemen were having a great natter over a fence and became chatty with us after exchanging a *bonjour*. They commented on how lovely it was to see the sunshine. Well, so Steve told me. I didn't have a clue what they said. I needed to get myself booked into French lessons immediately. I would ask Siobhan to give me the name of the person she said had taught Doug to speak French. I pitied the

French tutor who would take me on as a pupil. I was so impatient to be fluent there and then, not in a year or two's time.

Two days later we met the farmer next door. The postie came to the door to drop off the mail and to say welcome then Steve's golf clubs turned up via a delivery man. Mid-morning we drove to the local *tabac* (bar/café/lotto shop) for a coffee where we met Serge, the elderly owner. He didn't speak a word of English but Steve managed to exchange a few sentences with him. We'd only been back at the house five minutes when 'Gabriel the Gardener' turned up. Goodness, after the solitude of our first few days, it had definitely been a very busy and social morning. I struggled to just refer to him as Gabriel. He was always 'Gabriel the Gardener' in any conversation I had. The alliteration had a lovely ring to it.

Gabriel (the Gardener) then summoned me to discuss the kitchen garden. He took one look at my huge list of herbs and vegetables, rolled his eyes, grinning, as he muttered, '*Mon Dieu*,' and something else I didn't catch. Steve laughed and translated for me: 'And how much land do you think we have?' I may have slightly overdone it with what I would like in the veggie patch.

'We'll just have to buy a little more than we thought at the markets?' I volunteered.

'*Oui, exactement.*' Gabriel smiled, nodding in agreement. He seemed to be a very nice guy. He tried his English out on us and Steve practised his French with him; a very fair exchange, I thought.

So that was how our new life started unfolding. At that moment, though, my glass of rosé had disappeared and King of the Ride-On was emptying the last full catcher. He called out to me, 'Annemarie, what's for dinner? I'm starving.'

I rolled my eyes at him. 'Pigs' trotters in parsley sauce!' I retorted. That was my stock answer whenever he asked that question. Steve was always 'starving'. I heaved myself up from the table. It was time to be a good little French housewife and go and prepare my farmer husband some food.

---

1. Shorts.
2. A fictional character from the British soap opera *Coronation Street* whose name became synonymous with a tireless, working-class woman.

6

Settling in

Time was passing and we were starting to get into the swing of things. I was feeling so much better, eating properly again and my thinking was much clearer. We'd been out to Leclerc, the biggest supermarket chain there, and sorted out putting petrol in the car and how to pay. Down at the local town hall, we'd registered our presence in France.

It had been 'so far so good' with everyone we'd met. Henri, who looked after the French accounts for Mas de Lavande, came over to meet us. Although French, he was fluent in English.

'Cup of tea, Henri?' I suggested.

'Thank you, yes, that would be very nice. Where would you like to sit? Outside? It's still warm,' he said.

'Yes, lovely. Let's do that. I'll bring the tea out, if you want to make yourself comfortable in the meantime. I won't be a minute,' I said.

Once we were settled and the tea poured, Henri explained what he needed from us to keep proper records for Tristan and Richard.

'Do you use Excel? That would be the best way to record household expenses. Here's a debit card for the house. I'll put money on it when authorised by Tristan and after he's inspected the expenses each week. Do you understand me, Annemarie?' Henri asked.

'Yes, yes I do. That's no problem and, yes, we do use Excel so that's all fine, too,' I reassured him. 'I'll be keeping all the receipts and will have these clipped together for each week recorded on Excel.'

'Excellent!' Henri exclaimed. 'That's exactly what I want. Now, Tristan and Sarah have told me you would like an account opened at the Crédit Agricole bank. Is that correct?'

I didn't get the opportunity to say yea or nay as he continued, 'Because I've made an appointment for you. I'll send confirmation of time and date by email. That's settled then,' he said, closing the file. 'Now, there's an annual quiz night coming up. A lot of English come along. Would you and Steve like to come, too? It can be rather serious but it's good fun. My family is going,' he explained.

'Oh yes, we've been told about this. We would love to, thank you, Henri. That's very kind of you to ask,' I said, shaking his hand as he stood up to leave.

'Excellent,' he said again. 'I'd better get home. I look forward to working with you and seeing you at the quiz evening. Goodbye, Annemarie,' he added, waving to Steve on the tractor in the field.

What a nice man, I thought, heading back indoors to start dinner.

Siobhan arrived one morning with croissants in hand. While we sat devouring these with lots of hot coffee, she filled us in on how things ran at the property and gave us a list of the people we should contact for all the household needs. Siobhan also touched fleetingly on the previous guardians, telling us they'd wanted to go travelling before they left France. I felt so grateful towards Siobhan and Doug. They seemed super people and so willing to help us.

Once Siobhan had gone, I rolled my sleeves up, donned a thick pair of rubber gloves and tackled the oven cleaning in the main kitchen—twice. I'd need a Kango hammer to do a proper job. Next I threw out all the dry goods that had sat on the battered shelving over the winter. I scrubbed the shelves down with hot, soapy water and then sat down with pen and paper and a welcome cup of tea to prepare lists of the food required for the coming months. While I was busy in the kitchen, Steve was just through the doorway, cleaning out the sitting room fireplace. Andrea Bocelli kept us company while we worked, serenading us through the CD player.

Our lives started to resemble that of a local. Late mornings we visited our little *tabac* to buy our *flûte* (a type of baguette) for lunch. When I pushed open the shop door, the bell would tinkle and the warm, yeasty fragrance of newly baked bread was a mouth-watering greeting. Serge closed at noon on the dot for *his* lunch break and late one morning we arrived to a firmly shut door. Damn. We'd already missed him.

Jumping back in the car, we made a dash to the village for our lunchtime bread. We grew to love that little bakery, along with Antoinette, the woman who ran it. She would bring our coffee and *pains aux raisins* (spirals of raisin bread) out to the café table and spend a moment chatting. As time went on, she would come to greet us with the two-cheek kiss. Our village was a good size. It hosted a few boutiques, bank, hairdresser's, the bakery, the 8 à Huit (a grocery chain in the smaller towns), the *tabac* and several pizza places.

Luckily for us that morning, the bakery was still open. Most places had already closed up for the compulsory two-hour lunch break. Even the bank closed, too. With our still-warm *flûte* purchased, we drove around to explore a little more. We parked the car beside the hill-top church and cemetery and climbed to a gorgeous outlook. Looking down the lush, green valley, we could see over the orange clay-tiled roofs and chimney tops to church steeples in the distance and the surrounding countryside, dotted with sheep and some cattle. This was a very pretty, unspoilt area.

Back home and as soon as we'd swallowed our lunch we were straight back into more cleaning. By early evening, though, we'd had enough and chucked it in for the day. With a quick brush of the hair, and a little lipstick slicked on, I took myself out for fresh air with Steve. It was a brisk but easy walk to our *tabac* for a glass of wine and to see Serge again. We'd hoped to strike happy hour and possibly meet some other people. Not to be. We were the only ones there. Serge told Steve that people rarely came in for a drink. The *tabac* was principally a little grocery store on one side, with a little bar/coffee shop on the other. His chiller cabinets were full of mouth-watering cheeses and charcuterie. Our two drinks and 100g of Roquefort only cost €6.50. So incredibly cheap but I do have to mention it was the smallest glass of wine I've ever had.

We endeavoured to find something to watch on the old TV in the cottage but anything available in English was rubbish. Our friends from Auckland, Ginny and Dave, put us on to BBC Radio 4. We tuned into that on my laptop, listening to a fantastic episode of *The News Quiz*. Everyone was very witty and clever and it felt so good just to laugh and laugh.

Ginny Skyped me during those early days when I was utterly miserable. I poured my heart out about how I was feeling.

'You must phone Rebecca, my cousin, in Montpellier,' she said. 'Remember she's Michelin-trained and has cooked for large groups.'

'Why didn't I think of that?' I exclaimed. 'Thanks, Ginny.' For years, Rebecca had run a boutique hotel in the UK. So call her, I did.

Plans were made for Rebecca to drive up and stay for a few days. I knew she would be a great help in getting me started on creating menus and getting quantities sorted.

'Annemarie, I think it would be a good idea for us to visit

Leclerc while I'm with you,' she said over the phone. 'I can help you identify all the French equivalents of the products you use in New Zealand. I can show you which section they're in and what's best to use. What do you think?' Rebecca asked.

'That would be brilliant! Great idea. We'll definitely do that,' I agreed.

One year Rebecca had come to stay with Ginny in Auckland. She spent days preparing the most delicious *cassoulet* (a slow-cooked casserole of several meats and white beans) from scratch for a group of us. We loved her food and her company so Steve and I were both looking forward to seeing her.

With the house and grounds in better shape and Steve and I feeling more positive, we headed out to our first big market, in a town called Rabastens. We'd heard the market was very good. We didn't have GPS in the car but I was sure we would find it.

Rabastens is a large town and is home to Notre Dame du Bourg, a UNESCO World Heritage Site. It's a favourite weekend destination for residents of Toulouse and is on one of the pathways to Santiago de Compostela. This route is one which many people walk as part of their spiritual growth. They follow in the footsteps of St James, whose remains are believed to be interred in Galicia, Northern Spain.

7

Out and About

The Rabastens market was bustling when we arrived. Markets in France are a vital and integral part of the daily social strata and culture and mostly it's the older French who shop daily. Depending on the size of the town, there may be two markets a week. Every day there was at least one market to be found within an easy drive of our place. Access to these markets was often via winding, narrow country roads which were frequently only a car-width wide and meandered through tiny villages or hamlets. Each place had a church and a *tabac*, or some such enterprise, with four or five little houses clustered together. On our way to Rabastens, the views from the ridge fell away to rolling green pastures or bright yellow rapeseed fields. Farmhouses were dotted throughout. The majority of the houses were old like ours, with colourful shutters and no doubt a long history attached. Others were built in a more modern style: single-storeyed and box-like.

It was a very tranquil and relaxing drive—most of the time. That was until the day I locked eyes with a driver coming towards us. With Steve at the wheel, my right foot was pressed hard into the car floor, endeavouring to pump a brake I didn't have. My heart banged hard against my ribs as I shut my eyes and held my breath while passing the other car. When I did open my eyes I was surprised to see the side mirrors intact. It was a relief to be a few metres on, still on the road and not in the ditch.

I had yet to sit in the driver's seat. To become independent I needed to practise on the driveway. The whole prospect of actually driving myself scared me witless as the country roads were so narrow and the gearbox was very tricky. Well, it looked tricky, watching Steve trying to manoeuvre the damn gear stick into the right slot. I didn't have an issue with driving a manual car. It was driving on the right-hand side of the road while on the left-hand side of the car that was the problem.

We had coffee at a café a little further along the road from the market. It tasted so much better sitting out in the spring sun and watching all the goings-on. The market met all our expectations: full of beautiful fresh fruit and vegetables, cheeses, olives, dried meats, loaves of bread and fresh meat of every description, the most common being chickens with heads, beaks and feet still intact. This particular market had lots of vegetable seedling stalls.

'Steve, this will be a great place to buy all the seedlings we need, once the garden is ready,' I suggested.

'Sure is. It has everything we need. Have you got everything you want now? Shall we head off?' he asked, setting his empty cup down on the saucer.

In the car the sweet smell of the strawberries was so tantalising I popped a few in our mouths as we drove—absolute nectar on the tongue. When we arrived home, our bags were so heavy, full of glossy, vine-ripened tomatoes, crisp, dense heads of lettuce, tiny strawberries and plump, red raspberries. I couldn't resist buying the green beans and the vibrant carrots with their fluffy green tops.

The chilly start had turned into a gloriously warm day. By mid-afternoon, though, there was a terrific thunder and lightning show. The heavens opened, chucking down sheets of dense rain. Unable to do any outdoor work, Steve got started on our cottage and discovered what the bad smell was. He had pulled the oven away from the wall and spent the afternoon scrubbing behind and down the side of it.

'Yuk, Steve, I don't know how you can do it. I feel sick just looking at it,' I said, hurrying outside into the fresh air, retching.

Steve had a much stronger stomach than me. The wall was so thick with grease and the rock-hard contents of overflowed pots.

It was almost time to move from the *pigeonnier* into our small cottage. Before we could make the move, though, we had to wait for the gas man to turn up. The underground LPG (liquid petroleum gas) tank needed to be filled so we could cook, shower and heat the cottage.

Steve had found some old terracotta pots in the back of the barn and I'd potted two of these up with red geranium seedlings we bought at Rabastens. They looked very French and very charming as they sat either side of our French doors. I'd also washed absolutely everything in the cottage: sofa and cushion covers, curtains, towels and bed linen. Steve had hauled the mattress outside on several sunny days to give it a good airing. Everything would be fresh and clean for us when we did move in.

As the clock ticked over to 6 p.m., I returned to the cottage to see how Steve was getting on.

'I'm sure Serge must be missing us, Steve. Stop all this and let's go have a beer and another tiny glass of that delicious red wine,' I suggested.

With great relish Steve threw his dishcloth into the sink. He quickly washed his hands and grabbed his jacket off the hook. No need to ask him twice.

The weather was still a bit iffy so we jumped in the car and drove all of three minutes to the *tabac*. As we sat sipping and talking, the door was no sooner shut than it opened again. A lot of the locals were coming in for bits for their dinner. Everyone greeted us with a smile and a friendly *bonjour*. I'd learnt very quickly that you never entered anywhere without a smiling *bonjour*, a *merci* for any services received and never left without an *au revoir*. Living in the countryside was no excuse for sloppy manners. Politeness and good manners are a given in France.

Steve was being ruthless with me, making me practise my French. I watched the very polite Serge trying not to flinch, with his lips peeled back in a tight smile (really it was a grimace) as I uttered the words. I managed to tear his beautiful language to shreds asking for a glass of red wine. And then to top it off, Steve wanted me to understand the numbers when people told me how much things were. For heaven's sake! I ended up trying to interpret two very long-winded sentences. Translated, what I'd purchased was four euros 95. It all sounded like gobbledygook to me. It was too hard. I wondered how I was ever going to get to grips with the language.

The time-zone difference between New Zealand, Australia and France could be difficult to co-ordinate. Daylight saving adjusted at different times in each country but, finally, we made a connection with both our sons that evening. The 12,000 km distance reduced to nothing when we spoke on Skype. It made me feel a whole lot better to see and hear them. Because of the time difference, most people we contacted via Skype caught me in my dressing gown. Either I was just out of bed with sticky-up hair and no make-up, or at the other end of the day, in my dressing gown, hair not too bad but still no make-up—what a fright for them. Our boys didn't care.

8

A New Day

It was 8.15 a.m. and looked to be a gorgeous day ahead. The blanket of grey mist was lifting and the sun's golden and warming rays were starting to filter through.

Weeks had passed and Steve was coping very well having me in his life 24/7. When I mentioned this to him, I got a swift retort.

'Don't you worry. As soon as I think you're exceeding your female quota of 10,000 words a day, I'll be marching you down to the chicken coop to shut you in and you can chew their ears off.'

Hah, as if that would ever happen… So far, Steve didn't seem to have had a problem. I certainly didn't have a problem. I just kept on talking.

We'd fed the cats and released the 'girls' from their coop. Steve had refreshed all the straw in the coop the previous afternoon. The chickens had a delightful surprise when we tucked them into bed that evening, no doubt thinking they'd arrived for a splendid night at the Hilton. We crept up and had a peek at them around 9 p.m. but couldn't even see their crests, they had snuggled in so deeply. We could, however, hear happy, soft bock-bock noises from deep within. I knew we would have to fossick through to find the eggs in the morning.

The chickens loved to sun themselves outside the front door of the *pigeonnier*. After pecking around for a bit Maggie Hatcher would corral the girls together into a little huddle. Adele would finally shut up, Hilda stop scratching and Elle Macpherson cease preening. All of them would gradually sashay their little, fat, downy bottoms into the warm dust. With heads tucked under their wings, they enjoyed a mid-morning siesta. Peace reigned. I loved watching them. Who knew chickens had such personalities?

Rebecca was due to arrive and we were to drive to the next village to meet her. What do you cook for the extraordinary chef coming to stay? Something quick, easy and delicious, I was thinking. Maybe roast a chicken with lemon zest, garlic and herb stuffing. I could put tiny potatoes to cook alongside it and make a salad of baby cos, rocket and shaved parmesan. This could be washed down with some pale, dry rosé or a little Chablis perhaps. I'd bought some Roquefort and Comté cheese for afters and a delicious duck pâté to have with a drink before dinner. We were hoping the sun would still be out so we could sit at the little café table outside our French doors to enjoy our feast in the evening sun.

Talking on the phone with Rebecca about menus had given me a little more confidence. Her response when I told her that I was hopeless at making pastry was 'well just buy it, darling! Why put yourself through all that stress and bother?' Excellent advice, I thought.

We were still living in the *pigeonnier* but decided to unpack fully anyway and hung everything in the ancient armoire or tucked things into drawers. With the warmer weather, I was now out of my jeans and thermals and into shorts and a T-shirt. After hauling so many clothes halfway around the world, I looked at them hanging there. I did wonder if I would ever get the chance to wear them all. I knew I would enjoy putting on a dress, mascara and lipstick to greet new visitors. Now, finally, after a lot of hard work on Steve's part, our cottage was starting to look, feel and smell clean. Once Rebecca had gone, we would move in.

It was time to get Rebecca's room ready and throw open the windows to the spring sunshine and fresh air. I needed to make up the bed and plump the pillows so all would look comfy and cosy. The roses growing around the front door were blood-red and perfumed. I knew they would look beautiful in a vase and smell divine sitting on her bedside table, ready to welcome her.

9

A Special Visit

We were late leaving to meet Rebecca but we'd agreed to meet at 12-ish so I wasn't too bothered. I'd neglected to say to her we should meet at 8 à Huit. We arrived a little after midday and Steve walked the pavement so Rebecca could see him if she drove through. I popped in to say hello to Antoinette and to buy bread to have with our lunch of cheese, ham, rocket and tomatoes.

Steve spied Rebecca already perched at the outdoor table of one of the cafés with a coffee in hand; she'd beaten us to it. So after hugs and kisses, we sat and enjoyed a quick catch-up and our own coffees. I jumped into Rebecca's car and we followed Steve in the Citroën back to the farmhouse.

'Lovely. So lovely,' was all Rebecca could say as we came down the drive. The exterior of the house and surrounding fields and valleys *were* very lovely. It was a glorious day and this enhances any location. Once Rebecca had unpacked and settled into her room, we sat down to lunch. She was keen for a tour of the main house so as soon as we'd finished eating, we went over.

I was very curious to know what was in the huge, wooden box Rebecca carried with her. All was revealed as soon as she lifted the lid when we got back to the cottage kitchen. This precious box contains her recipes and is her travelling 'bible'. Rebecca kept flicking through the cards, pulling one out here and there. 'Oooh, yes, perfect,' she'd say when she spotted a recipe she thought would work for a crowd and put it to one side. She gave me some great recipes and ideas for lunches and the afternoon flew by as we discussed everything. When I looked up at the clock, it was already 5 p.m.

It was time to open some wine and sit out in the garden to enjoy our platter of olives, pâté and terrine. Making a start on our dinner, Rebecca had me sear the chicken on both sides before placing it on top of the tiny potatoes. I'd pulled rosemary and thyme from the garden and combined with some softened Normandy butter, stuffed these under the skin to add to the flavour. Once ready I sprinkled everything with a good glug of olive oil, salt and pepper and slid the dish into the oven. The food would look after itself while we nattered and enjoyed our aperitif.

Dinner was delicious and tasted even better eaten out in the evening sunshine. The cats and chickens lingered, hoping we might toss small morsels of the delectable chicken their way.

The next morning Rebecca and I left Steve and Gabriel toiling in the kitchen garden. After a bitter winter, lots of plants had died. The men were busy with the rotary hoe, churning through the compacted soil and replacing rotten boards in the border edging. Rebecca and I took ourselves off to the large Leclerc supermarket and worked our way through the various aisles. As we walked, Rebecca pointed out the products I needed to buy to get the best results from my cooking. She explained what was what while I furiously wrote notes. I didn't want to miss a thing.

Rebecca decided we would spend the afternoon cooking in the house kitchen. We gathered together the ingredients for a chocolate terrine. *Mon Dieu*! Only the best butter, cream, sugar,

80% cocoa solids chocolate, free-range eggs and cocoa were going into this dessert. Rebecca knew her cooking methods through and through so naturally she only used the best ingredients.

I reminded myself that I was under the tutelage of someone who was Michelin-trained and had worked in some fantastic restaurants.

What an exercise it proved to be. Rebecca dropped a half-dozen carton of eggs on the floor. We slopped the coffee/hot water mixture everywhere and we must have used most of the bowls in the kitchen. Heavens! It was such a fuss to get all the ingredients ready to go into the bowl.

'You must work fast,' she coached me, interspersed with 'no, no, no, not like that, like this!' Grabbing my whisk or spoon, Rebecca would show me how, hand it back and move behind me, encouraging me with 'now, come on, again, Annemarie. Try it that way.'

It was nerve-wracking working with Rebecca watching but not once was she patronising or critical; it was all well-meaning and I learnt a lot. I smoothed the top of the last chocolate terrine and the three loaf-tin moulds, filled to the brim, were ready for the freezer.

Rebecca talked me through quantities and what to make that could be pre-prepared. That way I would only have to focus on the main course in the evenings. Things like desserts I could pull from the freezer as and when necessary. She suggested parfaits, coulis, sorbets and ice cream and tart bases. Other items, too, such as pastry canapés which would be perfect to have with a drink. Everything could go from freezer to oven.

Our dinner that night was a leek quiche, made from leeks from the kitchen garden, with salad. The leftover cream, nutmeg, the rescued eggs, ground black pepper and a pinch of Camargue salt were all thrown in. Rebecca had me sweat the leeks in butter on low for at least 20 minutes which brought out the sweetness. The quiche was magnificent—rich and creamy, homemade and just delicious. The very naughty leftover terrine was our dessert. God, it was so good but so bad. A minute on the lips, six months on the hips.

The next morning Steve and I had our appointment at the local Crédit Agricole. As arranged, we needed to sign documents to get our French bank account opened.

'Rebecca, we'll only be 15 minutes. Why don't you grab a coffee at the *tabac* around the corner? We'll catch up with you there,' Steve suggested, as we were about to go into the bank.

Fifteen minutes was an understatement. Our meeting was with Monsieur Jacques. I'd assumed we'd be dealing with a man of 60 plus. Instead a very charming young man greeted us. He was about 23. I couldn't help but think of our sons as I couldn't visualise either of them working in a country bank at that age. City life was far more exciting for them. Monsieur Jacques was very efficient but we envisaged smoke pouring from the printer as reams of documents spewed forth. One hour later we left, wrists limp from signing all those pages. We found Rebecca happily ensconced at the *tabac* with coffee and the local papers.

By 9 a.m. the following day, Rebecca had packed her car and was ready to start her three-hour drive back to Montpellier.

'Thank you so much for everything, Rebecca. You've been an amazing help. I feel so much more confident now about dealing with the crowds and what to offer,' I told her, through the open car window.

'I've loved my little sojourn and it's been my pleasure. You'll be absolutely fine,' she said blowing kisses and waving into the air, she disappeared down the drive.

It had been great to have her company and advice. As time went on, though, this new-found confidence would be gradually whittled down to zilch by unforeseen events.

※ ※ ※

I was feeling guilty at the lack of work done in the house during Rebecca's stay. It was time to get moving again so I made a reluctant start on the linen inventory. There was so much of it; all in different sizes and states of repair. If it had been my decision, I would have thrown most of it out. I wouldn't want to be paying a fortune to sleep in some of those sheets. Steve was busy clearing out the barn and making a huge pile of rubbish to take to the rubbish tip. By 5 o'clock I'd made a significant dent in the inventory. My arms ached from holding up sheets to inspect, refolding the good ones and placing them in size order on the armoire shelves and putting the bad ones into a pile for Tristan to inspect when he was down. I crossed the landing and hung out of one of the second-floor windows, calling out to Steve.

'Hey, you, had enough for today? Let's go exploring for a few hours, while it's still light. Let's see where we end up.' I got a thumbs-up.

Steve was quite happy to pull the door shut on his clean-up. Off we went, meandering through villages and then down onto the main road. Taking an offshoot we climbed through an avenue of budding plane trees, following the road up the hill and into a new village. We parked and walked, craning our necks to look up at an ancient château, set high on a very steeply pitched wall. The café-bar across the square was open and had a very inviting, shady awning. A cold beer and glass of rosé were very welcome. It had been a glorious day of 30°C or more and it was still heavenly at 6 p.m.

Our day ended outside at our little table back at the house, eating a leisurely dinner of leftovers. Afterwards we just sat, enjoying the evening warmth and watching the sun set. There was no need for conversation. The only sound was the occasional click of crickets and the birds chattering, coming back into the trees to roost for the night. I'd put the chickens to bed before dinner. Steve stood, stretched and yawned.

'I'd better finish off the weekly report. You've done your bit, haven't you?' he asked.

'Yes, all sorted,' I replied, stacking our plates and glasses and ferrying them back inside. Half an hour later, the report was finished and emailed off. We fell into bed, whacked.

10

Phrenology

On the evening of our quiz, I was giddy with excitement about dressing up and going out. I'd coaxed Steve out of his beloved stubbies and T-shirt and he looked very nice in a dress shirt and casual trousers. I'd put on a pretty floral top, summer pants and wedge heels, swished my eyelashes with mascara and pouted the lips to add a layer of lipstick. Steve grabbed a bottle of wine from the fridge and we were on our way. Woohoo!

Siobhan had emailed us instructions how to get to their place; not the usual 'take this street, turn left into…' but more like 'when you see the concrete bunker on your left-hand side, take the right hand bend, then at the fork…' There were no street names in the country, only landmarks to guide us.

Pulling up at Doug and Siobhan's, we could immediately see we were so overdressed. Steve rolled his eyes at me.

'Bloody hell! I told you no one would be dressed up,' he muttered out of the corner of his mouth.

I was a bit embarrassed. Everyone else was in jeans, T-shirts and sneakers. As we got out of the car, Siobhan grinned at me as she leaned in for the two-cheek kiss to welcome us.

'Not to worry,' she laughed. 'You were always going to stand out as the "foreigners".'

That was lesson number one. Locals didn't dress up for *anything*. At the garden table, we met Doug's aunt and uncle who were passing through on their way to Italy, as well as Doug's dad, Doug Snr. He'd moved to France to be with the family about three years ago, after his wife passed away.

Dinner over we all bundled into cars and drove the country lanes to the local community centre. Once the quiz was underway, there was to be no chatting or mingling. This was a serious business and talking was only permitted during question breaks. I sat with Doug's aunt and uncle and Doug Snr and we managed to sneak in a few words of chat now and again. Questions were being fired off in both French and English. There was a great mix of both cultures as many English people had settled into the area over the last 20 years or so.

As luck would have it, the winning table happened to be the one Steve was sitting at. His cohorts were Doug and Siobhan and Siobhan's French friend Fabienne, a teacher. The award was a marble head, delineated by lines, dividing the various parts of the brain into different senses/functions. It's called phrenology. Steve has a fantastic memory and recall so with his brain, plus the other three brains in overdrive, there wasn't much chance of our table winning.

By the time we'd had a cup of tea and sampled a few sandwiches, it was very late and our drive back was along pitch-black country roads. Elegant, tall plane trees stood sentinel either side of the road, creating a guard of honour as we drove. The branches were pruned high up on the trunk and when approached in total blackout, the headlights captured eerie, X-ray images of bleached tree trunks and bare branches.

The whole evening had been fun. It was so good to have left all the hard work behind us and to meet up with people and relax for the evening. Our very first social occasion…even if we were overdressed.

11

Getting on with it

Our Sunday morning plan to explore the Saint-Antonin-Noble-Val market was thwarted as Gabriel had other ideas. He needed Steve to help him with yet more of the kitchen garden work and we couldn't exactly say, 'No, sorry, we're going out.' Nature's cycle dictates during the spring planting season. Gabriel was giving up his Sunday morning to get the work done and plenty of inventory work still awaited me. I left the boys to it and trudged up the path to the house to carry on counting and sorting the linen. I needed to make a start on the kitchen inventory, too. Several hours later hunger had sent Gabriel home to eat. With his own lunch out of the way, Steve mounted the ride-on mower once more to complete another circuit of the lawns. This was an endless task with constant spring growth.

Our cottage lacked quite a few essentials and we were about to go to IKEA in Toulouse to suss out what we needed. Just thinking about having to wrestle the busy motorway sent me into a spin and I wasn't even driving. The lanes appeared narrower to me than ours back in New Zealand. The speed limit is 130 km/hour, with the nerve-wracking bits being the lane-changing, taking the correct exit and being overtaken by others doing 160 km plus. It was over an hour's drive and through a toll road to IKEA. I can't explain why, but I was so anxious about it and we hadn't even left the property.

We used Fifi La Trixie Belle, our GPS, to get there and she was so helpful. Our afternoon disappeared as we purchased new mosquito nets and other bits and bobs. I checked out the wine and water glasses, too, knowing how bad ours were, photographing them and making a note of prices. Dining chairs and a coffee table were also on the list for the cottage. They would make the place more habitable and comfortable. The IKEA website doesn't always show everything so it was good to go and see for ourselves and price up what we needed.

On the way home, we stopped at the B&B down the road. In early summer the house would be full of the artists' workshop participants and there wouldn't be enough beds at the farmhouse to sleep all the guests plus staff. These workshops had been launched by Tristan to try and encourage more bookings at the farmhouse. It would be the first time Mas de Lavande was rented out on a commercial basis.

The B&B looked inviting as we pulled onto the gravel drive. It, too, was built in the local cream stone but this one had chocolate-brown shutters. Terracotta pots filled with red geraniums sat along one sunny wall. It looked immaculate. The barking dog alerted Madame that visitors had arrived. She came out of the front door, smiling, to greet us and introduce herself. Her name was Francine and she showed us through her simple but homely rooms. These would work well for our overflow. We promptly booked two rooms. We had no idea who would be staying but were informed that two extra rooms would be needed.

Steve's French was so good and so useful. He didn't think so but he was starting to hold full conversations and people understood him. The French sometimes speak so fast so at times, he did have to ask them to please slow down but no one seemed to mind. We always prefaced conversations with the fact that we were New Zealanders and our French wasn't the best. The young man at the checkout at the 8 à Huit store was very excited to learn we were from New Zealand. He was keen to tell us how much he loved to play and watch 'huuuuurghby' and wanted to go to New Zealand one day. It looks 'verrrrry beauuuuutiful'. He was in his early 20s and very sweet.

The next morning we saw Siobhan coming up the drive. In her hands were yet more buttery croissants, still warm from the bakery. I put the kettle on. Gabriel was due again to continue in the kitchen garden and a man was coming for the annual inspection of the septic tank. It had been very quiet at the farmhouse since Rebecca had left. Apart from the postal van deliveries, these little visits were the sum of our social life for the week but we were quite happy with the chickens and cats and our country life.

12

Fruit and Vegetables

Several days later Steve was absorbed in sorting out the barn, trying to get some semblance of order to the place. I was back in the kitchen. Now that the old ovens were finally clean, I had to check how well they worked.

While fiddling with the oven controls in the kitchen, I heard Steve come in through the garden door. He'd decided it was time to try the heating system in the main house to make sure it was working properly. He popped his head around the kitchen door.

'Hon, I've managed to get the heating going. With a bit of luck, it's all sorted but don't you worry about it. I'm off to feed the chickens. If I've done something wrong and the whole place explodes, you'll be dead. I'll be fine out in the garden,' he said with a stupid grin on his face. What a cheerful, loving thought from my husband.

'Gee, thanks!' I snorted. It was all I could muster.

The temperature gauge on the oven told me it had heated to 180 degrees. It was time to experiment with the cooking time. I slid a shallow dish containing our dinner of chicken legs, garlic, leeks, red peppers, green olives and capers into it, not forgetting the delectable little French potatoes. Fingers crossed it would cook OK.

The last of the winter leeks were now pulled from the garden. I'd finely chopped and sautéed these down in butter (as taught by Rebecca). They were deep in the freezer, ready for the first quiche. The strawberries were now jam (the first I'd ever made) and the onions were drying out in the sunshine, ready for use. How the jam would turn out, I wasn't sure but it had a great consistency when I poured it into the hot jars. Once I'd sealed and cooled them, I placed all the jars in the fridge to try to guard against any mould forming.

Steve had arrived back in the kitchen, having fed the 'girls' and completed the daily chore of cleaning out the coop. The heating was working and filtering through the house nicely.

'Oh good, you're still alive then and the house is still standing,' he said with a wry grin. He was more likely to be concerned about getting his dinner than worrying about my wellbeing. Dinner was ready and looked perfect—a good sign the oven was working properly. Steve poured our red wine and we sat down at the dining table in the main house to our delicious but simple meal.

It had been cosy and warm in the main house eating dinner but it was time to face the chill of the evening and walk back down to our cottage. Steve switched off the heating and went ahead. I set the house alarm, ready to leave, too. As I turned to open the back door, I could see through the little panes of glass that the cats were prowling around on the step. I just knew they were waiting to leap inside. We'd been caught before; when unlocking the house one morning, two of them shot past in a hurry to get outside. I had to search all the rooms to see if they'd left any deposits during the night. Opening the door just a fraction, I squeezed myself out so they couldn't slink past. With their plan thwarted of a night on a bed in the house, I knew they would follow me down to the cottage, wanting to jump on the couch and settle for the night. Alas Steve was with me so there was no chance I could smuggle them inside. They would be left outside for the night to fend for themselves, poor darlings.

The kitchen garden was looking fantastic, having been rotary-hoed by Gabriel, ably assisted by Steve. Between the two of them, they'd topped all the plots with mulch and had planted the first of the green beans. This was very exciting to see after all their hard work. It was only a matter of time before the tomatoes, courgettes[1], leeks, bell peppers, aubergines[2] and salad plants were dug in. All we needed was a bit of rain to get some growth underway.

It was time for us to do a little more local exploring. Late the following afternoon, we tootled down the drive and headed out into the countryside. We came across a few small but perfectly formed and pretty villages. It was yet another public holiday and everything was shut. People were making the most of the day, though. Farmers were sowing, others mowing, and some villagers were out walking or playing boules in the town centre.

We discovered a chocolatier that was open in one town and quickly pulled in.

'Fancy a pastry with your coffee, Steve?' I asked. I don't know why I bothered really. I already knew the answer. We shared an apple pastry and a delicious ball of the lightest, sweetest pastry which was dusted with icing sugar and oozed a light custard. Divine. They were the first naughty things we'd had, apart from a lemon tart left by Siobhan when we first arrived. OK, maybe they weren't the *first* thing. Oh yes, and we'd indulged in Rebecca's leftover chocolate terrine.

Steve's working life now revolved around the weather. Each evening he'd check online what the forecast was for the next day. It looked as though we were in for a cold snap. By this time we'd taken up residence in our cottage. There was only a thin quilt on the cottage bed to keep us warm so I borrowed the lovely feather and down duvet from the *pigeonnier*. The cottage windows and doors were double-glazed, which made a huge difference to the warmth of the place, but a cold wind still insinuated its way in through the cracks in the French doors. Just one more thing that needed fixing.

----

1. Zucchini.
2. Eggplants.

13

Touring

Sunday morning dawned and with cats and chickens fed and watered, I was getting excited. We were going away—for the *whole* day. Hurray! After tossing one indignant cat out that had snuck in, we locked the cottage door behind us and started our day trip. Steve had to revert to the time-old method of using maps. Fifi La Trixie Belle had fallen from the windscreen, smashing her screen. That was a short-lived and expensive buy so we would now have to get a new GPS, one week after having purchased the first. I hadn't fastened it securely in the first place and it had smashed on my kneecap when it fell.

Our first stop was Bruniquel, one of the many medieval hilltop towns in this region. It has a very steep climb from the car park to the château. You could do a guided tour of Bruniquel for 4€, although we didn't. It was a wet, miserable day and still there was a busload of tourists and another pulling up as we left. I could only imagine what it would be like in the height of summer: an absolute bun fight trying to get a parking space.

Next stop was the market at Saint-Antonin-Noble-Val. This beautiful town sits at the entrance to the gorges of the Aveyron River. Graceful, arched bridges cross its span at various points. It is home to the Roman House, the oldest secular monument of

France. There was plenty to see and do here but given the weather it wasn't a great day for us to go exploring. Other marketgoers were sheltering under umbrellas and awnings, it was so wet. Despite this it was still very busy. Stallholders shouted the quality of their wares, trying to entice people to taste and buy. Amongst the shoppers, we could hear a lot of English spoken, mixed in with French, Dutch and German.

Delicious aromas and visual feasts took us from stall to stall. The smell of Toulouse sausages and other varieties cooking wafted through the market, drawing us further in. These, together with peppery wild rocket, luscious red tomatoes, aged Emmental and creamy blue Roquefort, green beans, courgettes, garlicky salami and a *flûte*, completed our purchases. I went a bit overboard. The market was well-known for its produce, location and the village that surrounds the square as Saint-Antonin-Noble-Val featured as the setting in the film *The Hundred-Foot Journey*. When I watched the movie at the cinema a few years later, it reduced me to tears, reliving our time there.

Steve and I crammed ourselves into the small, steamy central café with the locals and their wet dogs. It was far too wet to be out under the very large plane tree in the town centre. It was my first truly delicious coffee since arriving in France. I sat back, cupping my hands around the warm mug, enjoying every last drop.

The rain stopped; patches of blue sky appeared and the sun came out. Back out on the street, Steve pulled the umbrella down and we continued our walk through the narrow back streets of the town, stopping to browse in the second-hand store. I was hoping I would find some nice chairs for our dining table or an interesting painting. Nothing took my fancy but Steve had been seduced by the selection of sweets in the sweet shop window. Unbeknown to me he'd made a secretive little purchase.

We devoured our picnic lunch of bread, succulent sausage, sweet tomatoes and blue cheese (rounded off with a bonbon or two) in the car, outside Cordes-sur-Ciel. We kept a plastic cutting board, napkins and a knife in the back pocket of the car seat for such occasions—very handy for impromptu picnics.

The village of Cordes-sur-Ciel is recommended on the tourist trail and is very popular. It came to life in 1222 and is yet another of the fortified, hilltop towns in the area. It was first known as Cordes (meaning rocky heights) but was changed as recently as 1993 to Cordes-sur-Ciel to indicate its height above the clouds in the low-lying areas of the valley below. Sadly we didn't have time to explore so only drove past and had to leave our visit until another day.

Next stop was Albi. Albi is home to, and dominated by, Sainte-Cécile Cathedral, the largest brick cathedral in the world. It's also home to the Toulouse-Lautrec Museum, housed in the beautiful Berbie Palace. On the lower level lies a pretty, formal parterre garden. I wished we had time to explore Albi as it looked very attractive, with a combination of the old and new. Maybe another day.

After our long day out, dinner and a short walk, it was time for bed. Coming out of the bathroom, I went to turn the light off. I could hear tapping on the glass and as I turned to see what it was I caught sight of two beady eyes and a coxcomb through the French doors. Oh Lord! Maggie Hatcher and the brood had come looking for us. We'd forgotten to feed them and to lock them in the coop, away from prowling foxes. Sliding into my sandals and stepping outside, I managed to artfully side-step a little deposit one of them had kindly left on the doorstep. Ah the joys of country life.

14

French Faux Pas

As we lived at the end of a long path, away from the drive and also with double glazing, we never heard people or vehicles approaching. It was rather a shock, and very disconcerting at times, to look up to find someone standing at the French doors, looking in at us. I learnt very quickly to put my dressing gown back on after a shower before taking the two tiny steps from the bathroom door to our bedroom door. It seemed unnecessary but one Saturday morning, I nearly got caught naked by Gabriel. He arrived at 7.30 a.m. to spray the roses. We just didn't hear him. Both Gabriel and I would have been mortified if he'd caught me *au naturel.* Same with the security alarm guy the previous week. There he was, standing at the door. There would certainly be no frolicking naked through the fields or skinny dipping in the pool where we were living. I would have died if someone caught us.

One Friday night Gabriel arrived at our door at about 9 p.m. It was fine; Steve and I both had clothes on and were doing the dinner dishes. He'd brought over a lot of new plants and seedlings that he wanted Steve to take care of over the weekend. Gabriel stressed more than once to keep everything away from the beady-eyed chickens. They apparently loved salad.

He needed help to unload the van so Steve and I trudged up the gravel path to give him a hand. As he lifted each plant from the rear of the van, he said the herb name in French and then attempted to use the correct English word. When he struggled with the name in English for a particular herb, he would put it under my nose for me to smell and I would say the English word for him. The basil duly came out and I said to Gabriel, 'Mmm, delicious. *C'est* basil. *Je t'aime, Gabriel.'*

He looked at me, aghast, turned several shades of pink and looked away with a silly smirk on his face. Steve had a stupid grin, also, and with my head swivelling from one to the other, I asked 'What, what? What's so funny?'

Steve could hardly contain himself. 'You've just told Gabriel you love him, you goose.'

Oh no! Poor Gabriel. We all started laughing. I was sure it wouldn't be my last French faux pas. Steve had warned me to be very careful with addressing and thanking people. It was much better to leave off the *madame* or *mademoiselle,* rather than give offence to some young girl by calling her *madame.*

Later that week, just as I had put dinner on the table, Steve came hurrying through the front door. 'You'd best get up to the barn and take a look. Flossie's given birth to three little kittens,' he said. That was a shock. Covering our food with a tea towel, I scooted up the path.

Flossie was the tiniest cat; a teenager herself, we thought. We had no idea she was pregnant, as she was so small. The other cats ganged up on Flossie for some reason and would always chase her away as soon as the food arrived. I wanted to make sure she felt safe where she'd given birth. I pulled a couple of hay bales around Flossie and her kittens, making cooing noises and stroking her head while she was feeding and then left her to get on with it. Steve had brought her food to her so she didn't have to leave the little ones. Flossie was being very spoilt. Dinner time for the cats was usually a mad, hissing, feeding frenzy at the best of times.

We had five miserable days in a row of endless, gloomy, wet, windy weather. It was cold at night but not so bad during the day. At long last there came a break in the rain. As we hadn't been anywhere apart from the supermarket and had been working solidly, we needed to chase our cobwebs away. We pulled on our boots and walked up to see Serge. This time I decided to buy a bottle of wine which Serge could leave on his shelf for me. I would slowly drain this (remember the glass size he used was like a large thimble) during our future visits. Steve had been trying local beers at Serge's little *tabac* and was enjoying a different one each time we went. That night it was like Grand Central Station in his *tabac*. We must have said *bonjour* or *bonsoir* to four different groups of people. It was 6 p.m. and the locals were fetching whatever it was they fancied for dinner.

Steve's French was proving invaluable. He was spending hours locating and phoning people in an endeavour to have an apiarist come. There was a large beehive in the sitting room chimney that we needed to get rid of. It was a common problem. We also needed to book the cats into the vet for their annual inoculations and get hold of the building company.

Some of it ended up a comedy of errors. Steve made a trip to the vet to collect cat boxes, only to find the surgery closed—a misunderstanding on the phone over opening hours. He made a second trip for the boxes later in the afternoon only to be told, 'Oh no, we don't keep them here. I'll have to bring a couple in. You'll have to come back.' Another misunderstanding!

He made a third trip a few days later. Luckily the vet was only ten minutes up the road. The horrible, stressful bit was going to be getting three very jittery, semi-wild cats into the boxes. I could imagine the yowling and howling in the car as they tried to claw their way out. I thought it would be extremely sensible for me to be very busy when it was time for the visit to the vet.

Steve arrived back with *one* cage from the vet, thinking he was going to fit three adult cats into that. Well, that was never going to work! There we were, the two of us hunched over, creeping along the path after these semi-feral cats, calling, 'Here puss, puss, puss.' Each time we bent that bit further down to grab one, off it would trot. We must have looked hilarious. But hilarious wasn't in Steve's vocabulary that morning. The air was blue as the frustration of two days' trying to get these cats sorted set in. Once we'd decided it was hopeless, we came up with the cunning plan for the vet to come out to us at feeding time. It was more likely he could grab each one by the scruff of the neck then vaccinate them. Steve drove off, seething I might add, to return the empty cat cage to the vet and to request a visit from him that evening.

Around 5.30 p.m. a van rolled up the drive and the vet got out. He was gorgeous. He looked about 20 but was probably more like 35. Armed with the necessary injections, he was ready to get to work.

I looked at Steve and mumbled, 'Right, well I'm not going to watch this fiasco. *Bonne chance* (good luck)!'

I headed off back to our cottage to prepare dinner. Less than ten minutes later, I poked my head out the front door to see the vet's van disappearing down the drive. Gosh, that was quick! However, Steve was walking towards me, one arm held away from his body, dripping blood as he went. He was livid.

'Well, that was a waste of effing time and money! Not one cat got vaccinated; we couldn't hold them and they took off in all directions,' he muttered in disgust.

I had the devil's own job keeping my lips pressed tightly together to stop my grin spreading across my face. I solicitously administered first aid to my husband's weeping gashes —poor man.

Speaking of medical matters, we had a very different experience on our first visit to see a doctor. The local doctor's hours were Tuesday afternoon, Wednesday morning, closed

Wednesday afternoon, Thursday afternoon OK, Friday morning OK, oh and by appointment on Saturday morning 9-11 a.m. Not a huge 'window' there. This is, of course, exaggerated but it went something along those lines. Patients didn't make an appointment during the week but turned up at the front door, pressed the buzzer and entered. Other patients looked up, muttered *bonjour* and then returned to their reading material. People found themselves a seat and awaited their turn. There was no receptionist. Once seen by the doctor, he/she informed you of the cost and proceeded to get out his/her cash tin and notebook. You paid appropriately and left, ensuring you said *au revoir* to those remaining in the waiting room. The process was terribly civilised.

We were having endless problems trying to get the Wi-Fi sorted. Not having much success talking it through over the phone, the specialist had to come to us. Mr Wi-Fi was English so there was no issue with our communication. Exciting! He was all done in 20 minutes, having ascertained it was a worn-out part. I managed to lure him into the kitchen, ply him with hot coffee and use up at least 5,000 of my daily word quota on him. He seemed happy enough to stay and chat; he was retired and wasn't very busy.

'So, Mr Wi-Fi Man. What brought you to France? The lifestyle, the weather?' I asked. Oh I should tell you Steve often refers to me as Detective Inspector Rawson. He thinks my conversations with people are more like an interrogation. That's so not true. I do ask a lot of questions but it's just because I'm interested in other people's lives. And I ask nicely.

'Well, Annemarie, I had a very stressful IT job. No one was surprised when I had a heart attack. I was overweight and did no exercise. I decided to chuck it all in and move to France. My wife was thrilled to do it. She loves France as much as I do.

We've been here for 20 years now and I've never felt better,' he said.

He gave us a list of restaurants to visit and wine cellars where we could get great deals on local wine and foie gras. One cellar he frequented put on an annual long lunch in the vineyard. It was by invitation only.

'You'll have to get to meet this vintner, Annemarie. Often there are more than 200 people in attendance. It's a magnificent occasion. The vintner sits everyone down, produces a delicious lunch, pouring glass after glass of his wonderful wine. We often sit there until early evening, enjoying the conviviality of it all,' he reminisced.

We'll have to get to know this man well, I thought. *I'd love to go to one of those lunches.*

Unfortunately he gave us other information that wasn't quite so welcome. Mr Wi-Fi Man had been coming to Mas de Lavande for several years. It was his turn to ask the questions.

'What brought you two to France, and to Mas de Lavande in particular?' he asked.

I told him all about responding to the advert on Gum Tree; how we, too, loved France and had done quite a bit of travelling and wanted to come back and work and live there for a while.

He smiled. 'And are you planning on staying long?' he asked.

'Well, for as long as we enjoy it here.' I explained the state of the place when we walked in and how shocked we were, but that we were getting on top of it now.

'You're the third lot of guardians I've met here. It's not an easy job, I gather,' he told us, suddenly preoccupied with his car keys.

'Oh?' My heart started hammering and I felt a chill creep down my spine.

'Rumour has it the previous couple walked out, taking only their basic belongings with them. It's rumoured *Monsieur* (Tristan), has a reputation for being difficult to work for. Other guardians never stayed longer than one summer, having worked all hours of the day and night with minimal reward,' he said.

Alarm bells were now ringing very loudly in my head. Steve and I looked at each other. It all began to make sense and reality started to dawn.

15

Working

Finally the weather had turned for the better and we were having longer and warmer days. Each morning it was a joy to push open the windows in every room of the main house, letting the warm sun and fresh air pour in. The wisteria vine was prolific and had entangled itself around the upper shutters and window frames. It was difficult to get some of the windows open and it took me half the day to cut it all back.

Gabriel was working all the hours God sent, not only at our place but for his other clients as well. It was his busiest time of year and there was so much work to do in our garden alone. I knew he was delighted Steve had arrived at the property and was doing the bulk of the work. He would arrive early and drive his van round to the shade of the big tree, close to the kitchen garden, and tune the radio onto the classical station. We all enjoyed the soothing music while he and Steve planted and I picked yet more ripe strawberries before the heat of the day gathered momentum. We had such a glut of strawberries, it was hard to keep up.

When Gabriel was with us, I would return to the house at about 10 a.m., fetch glasses of chilled water and a very strong plunger coffee for Steve and him to share. I'd fill the tiny, retro, gold and white filigree-patterned coffee cups I'd found in the back of a kitchen cupboard. They were so cute—the cups and saucers, not Steve and Gabriel. I even made pikelets one morning when Gabriel was there with his son, topped with *my* strawberry jam. They wolfed them down, calling them pancakes rather than pikelets and murmuring, '*Merci, merci,* Annemarie,' in between mouthfuls.

Gabriel had told us of a small market in a distant village that was pretty good. For a change we decided to go and get what we needed for the next few days from there. It *was* tiny but had all we needed: cheese, meat, fish, fruit and vegetables. The fishmonger we got chatting to had worked in London and Scotland and his English was very good. The fish looked so fresh, with clear eyes and the flesh white and firm. We got talking about salmon and how good ours is in the clear, cold southern waters of New Zealand.

'Here in France, never touch salmon imported from Norway. They spend their lives in one pond only and are never rotated through fresh ponds,' he informed us.

Which means it was only the one pond they swam and pooped in. In his opinion the best to buy was Scottish salmon. We purchased a couple of pieces of 'addock (as he pronounced it) from him for our dinner, which I egged and breadcrumbed. It tasted so good and just melted in our mouths.

It became imperative that I learn to speak French as I'd had my own series of misunderstandings. In the rush to leave New Zealand, I neglected to attend to some essential personal summertime grooming. Siobhan had kindly referred me to a day spa. On our visit to one market, we found the spa quite by accident. With my lack of French, I had to take Steve in with me to book an appointment.

The beauty therapist suggested Friday and thought she could fit me in at 4.30 p.m. What was it that Madame required? Steve struggled for the words in French and couldn't exactly interpret 'bikini wax' from the spa menu. We were both standing there, not sure what to do next while Mademoiselle patiently waited. To my horror Steve resorted to hand gestures, flapping his hands up and down around his crotch, trying to explain exactly what his wife needed doing. I was bright red at this stage and could have easily dissolved through the floorboards, watching Steve's antics. Poor Mademoiselle was looking very quizzically at Steve. Suddenly she understood and a discreet but amused smile lit up her pretty face.

'*Ah, oui, oui. Pas de problème. Je comprends,*' she said. (Yes, yes. No problem. I understand.)

With great relief we left with my appointment slip in hand with the time, date and day on it.

Come the Friday I had to verbally haul Steve off the ride-on mower as we were going to be late for my appointment. He dropped me off outside the door, right on time, and I went in. The young girl on the counter didn't speak English but we both smiled and exchanged a very pleasant *bonjour*. I gave her my name and she looked in the book and then shook her head. I looked in the book. No, my name wasn't there. That was odd. I was positive my appointment was for Friday. Next thing, out came a beauty therapist who did speak a little English. She, too, couldn't find me in the book. By that time I was feeling rather flummoxed with the language barrier. I made gestures, indicating that I would ring for another appointment and hurried out.

Once outside and around the corner out of sight, I rummaged in my handbag and found the slip of paper. The appointment was in another two weeks, not *that* Friday. What an idiot! Steve rolled his eyes when I met up with him and explained what had happened. He did laugh.

'Doesn't matter. We can get some shopping while we're here,' he said.

Two weeks passed. It was the same scenario all over again—scene I, act II. Steve had to stop mowing and park the ride-on mower. It was sweltering in the car. I'd made Steve rush through the shower but he was still very hot and starting to drip.

Halfway there I said to Steve, 'I'll get my appointment slip out and hand it to the receptionist when I go in. Then there'll be no confusion or Pidgin French from me.'

I glanced at it as I took it out of my bag. 'Oh, my giddy aunt, Steve! You won't believe this. The appointment was yesterday. I've missed it completely,' I confessed.

He was surprisingly patient. 'Well, we're on our way now. We'll have to go, apologise profusely and make another appointment,' he said.

Steve told me he explained to the therapist that he had a dumb blonde for a wife and we were very sorry. May we please rebook? No problem. I would go the next day... Now where did I put that piece of paper? He didn't really tell her I was a dumb blonde... He'd better not have!

Once I'd been appropriately attended to at the spa (on the correct day), we went in search of the local wine cellar recommended by Mr Wi-Fi. This wine establishment sold a particular red, which we were led to believe was very good, and at a very reasonable price. We sampled a couple of rosés and reds and bought half a dozen of the recommended Côtes du Rhône which was rather nice. I have to confess that we sank to a new low while we were there and purchased three litres of red 'Château Cardboard' for the total sum of 6€. I don't think I'd drunk cask wine since we were in our early 20s. While we sampled, customers were arriving with five-litre plastic containers, filling them with red wine via a hose through a hole in the wall, for the ridiculous price of 1.20€ a litre. The wine was supposed to be absolutely fine. Well, if you liked your reds a little rough, I'm guessing.

When shopping in Carrefour one day, Steve purchased a 1,65€ bottle of red to see what the lowest priced red in the shop would be like. It was astonishingly good (he said) so he went back and bought more for our own little 'wine cellar'. There happened to be a queue of French people behind him at the checkout. When they saw half a dozen bottles on the conveyor belt, several of them queried Steve about his choice of wine. Two then hurried off to the shelves at the back of the store to get some for themselves. It reminded me of the time we were in Bordeaux and our friend Kevin bought a 2€ bottle of wine from a butcher's shop. The rest of us had muttered to each other that we wouldn't be touching any of that. He could have it all to himself. But I remember him being pleasantly surprised at how good it was for the price.

As I knew there would be a houseful of guests over the summer, I needed to practise using the ovens and facilities in the main house. We decided to have a dinner party and invite those we'd met so far. There were eight adults and four children: Siobhan and Doug, their children, Siobhan's mum, Doug's dad, Henri and his wife, Bridgette, and their children. It was an enjoyable evening with us all around the table. For dessert I tried out Rebecca's lemon and orange tart with the strawberry coulis I'd made earlier and frozen. With the fresh strawberries on the side, it looked rather elegant and tasted divine. Everyone loved dinner and I was so pleased with how it had all turned out.

A few evenings later, we were waiting for Christian to arrive at the farmhouse. Christian was a chef from Cordes-sur-Ciel whom we'd found through Fabienne, Siobhan's friend. We wanted to chat with him about possible French cooking classes he might undertake for the Cornwall Art Club group. I started wondering if he'd remembered he was coming to us. It was getting on for 8 p.m. and we'd expected him at 6. It did cross my mind that perhaps he couldn't find the slip of paper he wrote the time and day on. Hmmm, that sounded familiar. He never did turn up that night.

16

Life in the Country

I discovered exactly how tough life in the country could be at times, especially when it came to animals and exactly how many mouths needed to be fed. Our little cat, Flossie, must have known her babies weren't long for this world. I was devastated to have to make an appointment at the vet to have her spayed and the kittens disposed of. It wasn't our decision to make as Tristan had instructed us to do it. It was horrible but a fact of life in the countryside. There were too many cats at Mas de Lavande as it was. The evening before the dreaded appointment, I came out of our cottage to go and feed the cats. Who should come trotting down the path towards me but Flossie, with one mewing, little white bundle swinging in her mouth. The storage door was wide open and I knew exactly where she was heading.

She stopped and I stopped. She glanced back at the barn, trying to work out which was closest— the barn or the storage area. She made a dash for the open storage door but I managed to cut her off and scurry her back to the barn. The little wretch swayed to and fro in her mouth as she ran. In her haste she dropped it halfway. I rushed to her 'nest' to check on the others but they'd gone. She'd hidden the other two in the storage area already. Flossie picked up her kitten and I stepped aside and let her run for the room. That way I would see where she'd put the other two, thinking they'd be tucked up in one of the old blankets in there. Alas, no. She squeezed through a tiny gap where the roofline angled down to meet the wall. There was no way either Steve or I could lie on our stomachs in that tight space to put our arm through the gap.

The next morning Flossie was waiting with the other cats for breakfast. This time we managed to grab her and put her in a borrowed cat bag before she could eat anything and bundled her into the car. No kittens of course. They were safely hidden in the wall. Off Steve went down the drive. Halfway down that drive, Flossie had somehow managed to wriggle out of the bag. She roamed all around the car, howling and yowling and climbing up on the dashboard while Steve tried to drive. He didn't have much luck with any of those cats. Flossie did ultimately settle and Steve got her to the vet to have her spayed; both of them returning alive.

The kittens would have to remain in the wall until they were old enough to come out by themselves. Then what would happen? I didn't want to think about it.

It was actually a bonus having the semi-wild cats. To my horror we'd discovered grass snakes, about ten centimetres long. One of the cats wanted to show us how clever she was and brought one to the front door. She was having a great time, tossing it up in the air then pouncing on it until it ended up punctured and pulverized. I shuddered, it was so revolting.

When Mr Wi-Fi Man had come to solve our problem, no money had changed hands as we didn't have enough cash. So we arranged to drop the money off to him as we were going to his village. He decided the easiest thing to do would be to put the money in an envelope and give it to Charlie who worked behind the bar at his favourite café. Charlie would pass it on to our man when he came in next. No problem. Afterwards Steve and I decided to go for a long drive through the countryside. Looking up from the main road, we could see what looked like a massive castle wall. Veering right we started climbing a long, winding road to a hilltop village called Puycelsi.

Through the trees we caught glimpses of the church steeple, with the village itself perched precariously on the cliff face and a huge stone wall surrounding the town. Arrow slits were cut in the walls and in centuries gone by, villagers would have fired from these at potential invaders.

The village of Puycelsi, with an amazing outlook over the Vère valley and the Fôret de Grésigne, was so very pretty. Armies would have been hard-pressed to storm that fortress centuries ago. There were sheer drops on all sides of the surrounding thick stone walls. We took our time wandering through the little streets. The small homes were so quaint, with little paned windows and matching painted shutters and doors. Each had pots of colourful geraniums and other flowers potted up in wrought-iron window boxes and at their front doors. Windows were open to the warm, late-afternoon breeze. While passing we could hear families talking or the murmur of a television. Some of the women sat, wearing their aprons, under the leafy, shady trees, passing the time of day with their neighbours while their dinners cooked.

One beautiful tourist spot in Puycelsi is the tiny stone church known as the Chapel of Saint Roch which has the smallest entrance door. Its history dates back to 1703 when it was first erected by the then inhabitants to give thanks to Saint Roch for protecting them from the plague. The chapel is now home to a visitors' centre, with plenty of information about the village and its surrounds.

Before we toured the streets, we'd parked the car to visit a café we'd heard a lot about. Steve ordered a small pitcher of rosé and a small bottle of mineral water for me, while he tried one of the many varieties of French beer. The heat was intense. It was getting on for 6 p.m. and we were very thirsty. It was shady and cool sitting under the thick canopy of green vines entwined throughout the metal framework overhead. Lots of people wandered in and out, locals and tourists alike. Everyone talked in desultory tones, a little drowsy from the heat. The scenery laid out in front of us was magnificent: a vista of deep ravines and dense forest, with the occasional house and church dotted amongst it.

Steve had a second beer while we discussed where to have dinner.

'Do you want to try the food here? There's a restaurant further up this road if you wanted to look at the menu there?' Steve asked.

We decided on the one further on as we waited for the bill. It was a hefty bill for two beers, a glass of rosé and a mineral water. Steve had chosen special beers and exclusive mineral water. We would have to watch that in future as we couldn't afford to blow our hard-earned euros on a couple of drinks out. After checking the prices of the restaurant, we decided to wait until we were a little more financially stable to eat out. Leftovers would have to do.

We'd been investigating more B&Bs and I'd sent out an email in French (thanks to Google Translate) to some local establishments. One couple that ran a place not too far from us decided to come and visit and introduce themselves. She was Dutch; he was French and we had a great chat as she spoke English as well. They were both very keen to have a look through the house. After the tour we sat out having coffee.

'The house is quite nice, yes,' she said. 'It will be even nicer once the bathrooms have been renovated.'

Steve and I snorted with laughter.

'You don't understand. This is how Tristan likes the

bathrooms. He calls it "rustic". I call it "very tired",' I explained. They were rather shocked that it was to be rented out like that. Me too.

As they were leaving, they extended an invitation for us to visit their B&B the next day. We were very curious to see their property. As we walked through it, we could see there was absolutely no comparison with Mas de Lavande. Theirs was quite modern, with lovely bathrooms. We sat down with a coffee at their outdoor table and talked together about how they ran the B&B. It was all food for thought. Maybe we could buy something and run it as a B&B? That made more sense to work for ourselves rather than for someone else for minimal reward.

A few weeks on, and after forfeiting dinner in Puycelsi, we decided it was time for us to have a nice dinner out. Having learnt that you don't dress up, we pulled on tidy jeans and tops, hopped in the car and drove into a nearby village. We knew of one particular restaurant as we'd got chatting to the French owner on one of our B&B-hunting exercises. His wife was alleged to be an excellent cook and made a great curry. This wasn't French haute cuisine but it was exactly what we fancied. Both of us bypassed the gizzard salad, snails and some other offal offerings and enjoyed a bowl of frics as our entrée, followed by a beef curry. It seemed wrong not to be eating something French but we loved our choices.

It was time to explore markets further away, not just the ones in villages nearby. The Montauban market is large and the day we went it was heaving, with throngs of people at every stall. We queued with them as we waited patiently to make our purchases. Every customer received the same solicitous attention. Standing there we observed many different cultures. One café we passed was filled with men sitting in the shade out of the heat of the day, their tiny cups of thick black coffee set in front of them.

Here they sat, chatting, while their womenfolk shopped. Steve and I gathered together what we would need for the next few days and wandered, enjoying looking at what was available.

'Look, Steve. Beetroot seedlings and a new type of basil with tiny leaves,' I said at one of the plant stalls. 'Let's buy some of these. They'll be ready when we have the artists' weeks. I could make that raw beetroot and carrot salad I do at home, for the health-conscious ones, anyway,' I suggested.

'We've got plenty of room left in the kitchen garden so get what you like. It'll add to the variety we can offer,' he replied. 'I'll put them in when we get home.'

Yum, I thought. I loved that salad.

One morning of note had been very exciting for us as we had a pre-arranged Skype chat with our friends Mike and Marion, Ann and Kevin, Cheryl and Greig and Dave and Amanda. They were all at Mike and Marion's holiday home back in New Zealand and in our honour Kevin was cooking a French dinner. With his gourmet skills, we knew there would be delicious and beautifully presented food on the menu, plus some amazing French wines. The first course, French onion soup, was held aloft for us to savour and supposedly smell. This was to be followed by duck with grapes, duck-fat potatoes plus vegetables. Dessert was poached pears with a chocolate sauce. I did hope a fragrant cheese course would be part of their dinner. Cheese must be eaten before the dessert, of course. That's the true French way.

They'd each dressed in a French outfit of some sort. Steve and I were to judge 'best in show' or, really, best French dressed. Most had donned the obligatory black beret and some had added scarves. Amanda had a red, white and blue wig on, claiming she'd had a disaster at the hairdresser's. Ann kept dropping her shoulder strap to give a sexy French look and Mike, with his greying beard, dark, swarthy skin and wearing a beret and scarf, could easily have passed as a Frenchman.

The best, however, was Cheryl who was dressed in fishnet

stockings, leopard-print shoes, a sleeveless red dress and what looked to be a fur jacket. Under her arm was a soft toy dog which she kept calling Fifi. We awarded her 'best dressed'. There were lots of rude gesticulations with French bread sticks throughout the Skype call and it became difficult to hear anyone speak, we were all laughing so much. They'd obviously had a few wines already; we hadn't as it was 7 a.m. for us. Regardless, it was fun to Skype and to see them all, even if the call was tinged with sadness. If we'd been in New Zealand, we would have been with them. A few tears were shed. I had to tell Steve to harden up and wipe those tears away… OK, OK, it was me crying, alright?

17

A Reality Check

The honeymoon was definitely over. The anxiety attacks I'd suffered at the beginning of this adventure had returned with a vengeance and I was questioning what on earth we were doing there. Well, I knew why we wanted to be there but it had become clearer by the day that we'd chosen the wrong place. Actually that's not correct. The location was stunning; the people we'd met were friendly and welcoming. We'd chosen the wrong people to work for. After giving 110% and receiving thinly veiled jibes, I found it increasingly difficult to be positive.

Steve and I were on the receiving end of some rather petulant and petty behaviour and comments. Communications with Sarah and Tristan were difficult and it often appeared as if they hadn't spoken to each other. Our instructions from both parties differed so often, we didn't know which way to jump. We just had to get through the negatives and I tried to stress less.

Weeks had passed in a blur, with both of us putting in some 12-hour days since we'd arrived. When we first got there, we'd seen a half-finished building behind the barn. Sarah had told us this was to be the artists' studio, with French doors leading out onto an outdoor terrace. However, there had been a few issues in getting it completed.

Tristan was getting very agitated and consulting anyone and everyone how the interior should look and what the finish of the exterior should be. Everything needed to be completed before the Cornwall Art Club people arrived. Project-managing the art studio completion wasn't in the job description but Steve was happy to oblige. He started with phone calls, leaving messages for the building company and the main contractor to try and find out when they would be back to finish it. His calls weren't returned and Steve couldn't understand why.

Steve was then asked to find companies to quote for the interior flooring and the terrace. It was first decided this would be polished concrete. Steve went on the internet to find appropriate contractors anywhere from Toulouse to Albi. He typed up in French what he needed to ask so the call would have some fluidity to it. This process needed to be done for each type of finish suggested. He then made the call and set up appointments for two or three of these contractors to come out and quote. It took time to get these appointments, then weeks for the contractor to get to our site.

Steve had to fit this extra work in around his daily chores and it took hours. He would leave a message on cell phones but no one called back, or it would be the next day, or we would miss the call entirely as there was no work mobile phone. It was challenging to manage. So should it be polished concrete inside and out or just the interior? Perhaps put down a timber floor inside and a plain concrete finish for the terrace? Maybe they should both be timber? What about underfloor heating for possible winter rentals? Steve just wanted a final decision to be made and a contractor engaged to do the job.

With all this work under his belt and thinking he was making headway, Steve would then receive yet another email several days later saying, 'No, I don't think we'll do that, can you...' This went on for at least another three weeks. It was doing our heads in. Unfortunately we had to do as requested and keep going.

After leaving three messages at the construction company, Steve finally got through to an actual person. He discovered the reason they hadn't returned to complete the building. It was for the plain and simple reason they'd not received payment for work to date, as originally agreed. What was the problem? No funds? If the art studio was to be up and running for the Cornwall Art Club group, these people needed to be paid. Steve had to get this resolved. As it turned out, the builders were an affable, hard-working team of four. Once payment had been made, they returned to site and often sweltered in 35-degree heat to get the job done in time.

It was emphasised to us often: Mas de Lavande was to be looking fabulous and picture-perfect for the art club group and the two artists' workshop weeks and also to be ready for the Art Auction Day at the end of summer. As part of our job description, we were going to play a major role in developing the property and garner interest in future rentals. This is what had excited us the most—to use our business skills to enhance and improve what was already there and to get Mas de Lavande advertised to the right clientele. The property did have 'great bones' but most definitely needed some interior work.

To this end I made a list of what I thought would make everyone's stay comfortable. I compiled a house handbook of how everything worked. Also listed were supermarket opening hours, the nearest village, different market days and times, emergency contacts and the local chemist and doctor. I spent hours in the evenings bringing the handbook together, making sure I had correct phone numbers, addresses and opening times. Steve had been busy, too, investigating locations of golf courses, wine tastings and cycling tours of some of the wonderful market towns and villages in the area. Finally the job was done.

I emailed everything through to Tristan and Sarah. Stony silence. When I look back on our time at Tristan and Richard's place, I doubt the handbook or the household inventory was ever looked at. As for my list of what was needed in the house; it was starting to grow because so much of the crockery was chipped and there wasn't one complete set of glasses. I was also desperate for new pots and pans in the kitchen. In some bedrooms moth-eaten mosquito nets needed to be replaced and we badly needed new towels and sheets. Most of the sheets were grey and getting very threadbare. I looked at each item from the viewpoint of 'would I like to sleep in that or use this?' If I was renting the farmhouse for a week, what would I expect?

Finally we got our wish for a work cell phone, something we'd repeatedly asked for. It arrived but only after Sarah had spewed a lot of unpleasantness down the house phone at us. Amazingly we received a verbal apology for the tirade. Steve was able to shrug it off but I was left stunned and upset by how vehement and nasty it had been.

18

Still Working

The spring weather had brought on a lot of pasture and crop growth. It wasn't unusual to look out into the black of night and see a bright yellow orb. It wasn't the moon but one of the local farmers, still on his tractor at 11 p.m. He worked through the night, using a powerful light on top of the tractor cab to guide him through the fields. Everyone earning a living from the land was caught up in the race to get the first crop of hay cut and baled before any rain came. It was common (and scary) to meet a tractor taking up most of the narrow road, with hay bales bouncing along on the trailer behind it. Once I started to drive, if I was caught behind one, I would keep my distance and just tootle along behind until it turned off. There was no way I was even going to *try* and pass them.

To be ready for the booked guests, we'd done an intense clean of bedrooms and bathrooms and made up the beds. There wasn't much hope for the kitchen but I'd done my best. At least everything was now hygienic and all the crockery, tableware and shelves washed and clean. Thank heavens we'd finished as we ended up with 24 hours' notice that a family of five were on their way. We wouldn't know until they arrived whether we were to be hosting or if they would take care of themselves. Whichever way it went, we needed to get some basics in.

Steve had taken Fifi La Trixi Belle into Toulouse to get fixed as he'd found someone online to fix her for 60€. This was a big bite into our meagre earnings but much cheaper than buying a new one. He stopped and did a quick shop on the way back. I added last-minute touches to the bedrooms and bathrooms and picked some wildflowers for the living room. The constant piles of dead flies and hanging cobwebs were such a nuisance but a quick vacuum saw to those and I was ready. We expected the family any time after 4 p.m.

By 7 p.m., I'd prepared a standard first-night fare of butterflied chicken sitting on the delicious little French potatoes, adding loads of garlic, olive oil, and sage and rosemary from the garden tossed through the lot. This was always a safe option, not knowing anyone's tastes and most children ate chicken.

The oven was heated and ready for me to pop the chicken in as soon as they arrived. Salad leaves were washed and crisping in the fridge. Steve had bought a couple of lemon tarts and I added strawberries from the garden for their dessert. I whizzed upstairs for a final check. All the lamps were on in the bedrooms to give a warm welcome. I'd bound towels, hand towels and face cloths with raffia and a sprig of lavender tied into the knot and laid them on the ends of the beds. Perfect. Everything looked lovely; well as lovely as I could make it.

I dashed down to our cottage to put something similar in the oven for our dinner and to check the emails. Lo and behold an email had come in from Sarah saying the family had decided to head for Paris straight away and wouldn't be coming. Aaargh! Why hadn't she called us on the phone? I was so frustrated. All that effort for nothing.

Steve, who had done a last skim of the pool, came in the door.

'Listen to this, Steve. I'm so annoyed!' I cried. I read out the email to him.

'Why didn't she call? We've got the cell phone now. What a waste of time,' he said querulously, just as exasperated as I was.

I stomped back to the house, bagged the chickens and packed them into the freezer. I snapped off all the lights, closed the windows and slammed shut the back door, locking it behind me.

Back at the cottage I said to Steve, 'I think this was where "must be flexible" written in the job description comes into effect.'

'Hah!' was all he could muster.

Steve and I sat down with a drink at our little table in the evening sunshine. I took several deep breaths, trying to calm my mind while waiting for our dinner to finish cooking. I couldn't believe it. By that stage I no longer trusted Sarah. I suspected she'd known for some time before she notified us that they weren't coming. Either she completely forgot to let us know or it was deliberate. We were definitely seeing another side to her.

The plus side was that the house and rooms looked good for the next guest who funnily enough was due to arrive around 11 p.m. that coming Friday night. He would be looking after himself in the cottage next door. No problem. That was ready as I'd given it a good clean when we moved into our place. Only the bed needed making up, the rooms given a light dust and a quick vacuum. When we heard our previous guests were no longer coming, I transferred over to the cottage the fresh milk, tea, coffee, muesli and yoghurts that we'd got in. At least they wouldn't go to waste. Steve and I had demolished the lemon tarts. Well, they wouldn't keep, would they?

Then with two hours' notice, we were told that two of Richard's lawyer friends, Philip and Peter, would also be arriving that same Friday evening, staying in the main house. They would be looking after themselves, too. Thank heavens for that as I didn't have any other food available and by that time, Serge's *tabac* was shut. We'd made up all the rooms and beds ready to go so there was no need to do a thing. Philip and Peter appeared very nice so we invited them to come and sit with us and have a glass of wine before dinner.

With Gabriel at Mas de Lavande so much, and his wife often helping in the garden, it was inevitable we would invite them for dinner. Over time we became good friends. Having dinner together at our place was an excellent opportunity for their eldest daughter to practise her English. They thought I could try and understand what they were all saying, too. Oh really? In reality I was starting to pick up more and more of what was being said. Regardless of the language barrier for us all, we had a fun evening. The girls loved the chocolate brownies and strawberry coulis I'd made, as did Gabriel who lifted his plate and pretended to lick it clean. I packed up the rest of the brownies for the family to take home. Steve and I sure didn't need to eat it even though Steve, through all the hard, physical work he'd been doing, had lost six kilos. He rarely snored now. Absolute bliss. No more scrabbling around in the middle of the night for my earplugs or for me to have such a disrupted sleep.

Once Gabriel and family had left, we waited and waited for the last guest to arrive. I couldn't stay awake any longer and at midnight I sent a message to Sarah, advising our man hadn't arrived and I was going to bed. I was shocked, given how late it was, when a message pinged back straight away saying she'd *just* been told it was *Saturday* night he was arriving. It was hard to believe that Sarah had 'just been told'. Maybe she'd got her days mixed up. It's easily done and if she could just apologise I might have been a lot more understanding.

Steam was starting to come out of my ears at the second no-show and the waiting up until midnight.

'Just how flexible are we supposed to be? Does it not register or matter to them the trouble we go to?' I raged.

'Obviously not.' Steve snorted. 'It's just so inconsiderate.'

'I'm learning fast that we're really just a means to an end. They employ us at minimal cost before summer to prepare the house and property. Then when people are here, we're to shop, cook, clean, do the garden, drive and be at their beck and call. OK, I get that but for heaven's sake, have a little thought for what we do to prepare for people coming to stay,' I fumed.

I was on a roll, letting all this frustration pour out.

'And what's going to happen when the weather turns to autumn and there are no more bookings? Say "thank you very much, but we don't need you any more"?' I continued.

'Come on, hon. Let's just go to bed. There's nothing we can do about it now,' Steve reasoned. 'Why don't we head out for the day tomorrow? Everything's ready for our man and he's not due in until 5 p.m. At least we could have a break and enjoy the countryside,' he cajoled, switching off the light and taking me by the arm.

Since our arrival we'd only had one full day off. However, that had been a familiarisation trip to Saint-Antonin-Noble-Val, Bruniquel and Albi so that we would know what to recommend to guests for their own exploring. Some days, once we'd completed our chores or mid-afternoon, we'd jump in the car to go and explore some of the little villages nearby. Tristan (no mention yet of Richard) was due to return to stay for a week or more so we definitely needed some downtime and to have some relaxation before we hit the ground running.

19

It's all go here

When the postie pulled up in the van and handed me an envelope all the way from New Zealand, I was very excited. Alex, a friend of ours back in Auckland, had sent a wad of her favourite recipes. These would be great to make for a crowd. I was looking forward to trying some of them, particularly the salmon, roasted red pepper and courgette pie. That would be great for an easy lunch with a salad added. The barbecued duck salad and fish with ginger sauce sounded tasty, too. There was plenty of delicious food to choose from and to make. The difficulty might be in sourcing some ingredients.

I'd been busy in the kitchen and had made up a double batch of savoury crêpes, some quiches and caramelised onions. These would be very handy to have in the freezer, ready to pull out at a moment's notice. It seemed that's all the notice we got at times. I also started to plan a week's worth of menus for those coming to stay. The recipes would be based around what would be ready to eat from the garden and what was going to be economical. Naturally they would need to be healthy and delicious as well. I was to submit this meal plan through to Tristan and Sarah the week before the Cornwall group arrived. I made the mistake of mentioning that I wanted to buy some ingredients so I could prepare things for the freezer to get a head start. This would mean time would be less pressured when guests were in the house. Once again the response was negative. Previous people cooking at Mas de Lavande had been more than capable of preparing everything on the day, apparently. Tristan told me it wasn't necessary to freeze anything. I'd started not to care or to listen and went ahead anyway.

Steve and I were in for a big surprise. Finally we were going to meet Richard, Tristan's partner. He was due to fly in the night after his friends Philip and Peter returned for another visit and would join them for a couple of days' relaxation at the farmhouse. The three of them would take care of themselves so I just needed to make sure his bedroom was perfect and the kitchen spotless. It would be interesting to meet him finally.

Philip and Peter arrived early evening. Steve and I had both enjoyed their company during their last stay as they were interesting and fun. Not only were they lawyers from the London practice but they were also big art lovers. The two of them would trawl around the second-hand markets on the hunt for old French artworks in the remote hope of finding a Gauguin, a Monet or something by another famous artist, pulled out of an attic.

'Hi, Annemarie, Steve, how are you both? We've picked up wine and some meat for dinner and wondered if we could come and join you to eat?' Philip asked, as he came down the path. 'It's such a gorgeous evening.'

'Hello, Philip. Great to see you. Yes, of course, come and join us. We'd love that,' I said, smiling at him.

'I'm about to barbecue. Want to throw your meat on here?' Steve offered, pointing at the burning coals.

'Fantastic! I'll whip up to the house and grab it and Peter

and we'll be with you soon. Thanks.' He stopped in his tracks and turned to me. 'Oh, Annemarie, isn't it great Richard's coming over? He definitely needs a few days off. It's been crazy in the office in London.'

'Yes, we're so looking forward to meeting him. He was out at a client dinner the night we met Tristan at their Richmond home so it's good that he can come and chill out for a couple of days. See you in a minute,' I replied.

Steve brought out another couple of chairs and organised them around our rusty little table. I quickly added to the salad bowl to make enough to share. The boys arrived with their bits and pieces. Philip joined Steve at the BBQ and it wasn't long before delicious smells were wafting across the table. Peter opened a beautiful bottle of Bordeaux red, sharing it around the four glasses, and plonked himself down next to me.

'Right, Annemarie, how's things? What have you been up to since we last saw you?' he asked, turning to me and lifting his wine glass to his lips.

Sitting there chatting, overlooking the valley, was absolute magic. The night came in and the only light illuminating the evening was from our table lamps, filtering out through our French doors. This light and the stars in a country sky were all we needed.

Late afternoon the following day, I was unpacking groceries in the cottage when I heard voices outside. Steve and Richard arrived at the door.

'Richard, this is Annemarie. Annemarie, Richard,' Steve introduced us. 'Richard came out to the vegetable garden to say hello so I thought I'd bring him down to meet you,' Steve explained.

We shook hands. 'Lovely to meet you, Richard. I'm so glad to put a face to the name and that you could get here for a few days to unwind,' I said. 'Would you like to sit down for a minute? Have a cold drink?' I offered.

Richard rubbed a hand over his weary face. 'I'd love to,

thanks, Annemarie. It's been so hectic at work and I'm really looking forward to some time out,' he said tiredly, pulling out a kitchen chair.

There was something really warm about Richard. I liked his casual dress style, too: cream shorts with a soft-pink, linen, short-sleeved shirt, and a pair of flip flops on his feet.

Richard stayed a little while, enjoying his beer with Steve, before leaving us and joining Philip and Peter up at the house.

'Well, what did you think?' Steve asked me once Richard had left.

'What a lovely man. I instantly liked him,' I replied. 'I'm pleased he was so easy to get on with. He seems relaxed and calm and really quite charming. And, Steve,' I added, turning to him, 'he looked us in the eye!' I winked, grinning.

The afternoon Philip, Peter and Richard were returning to London, Richard came to say goodbye.

'I just wanted to thank you both before I go. You've certainly made a difference to the place. The house and the garden are looking great. I hope to see you again over the summer,' he said, shaking our hands.

'Thank you very much,' Steve said, pumping his hand. I just beamed at Richard, so pleased to hear those words. 'It's been great to meet you and we look forward to seeing you back here, too. I'll come over and help you with your bags,' Steve offered, walking towards the house with Richard.

I sat down on the edge of the studio terrace, watching them go, and hugged myself. It didn't take much to make me happy and Richard's words had made me very happy. How completely different he was to Tristan.

One evening the chef from Cordes-sur-Ciel, Christian, emailed us to say he and his wife, Lisette, were having a lot of guests for a dinner party at his home. Could we please help them spring clean the house? Yes, of course we could, for a small fee. For five hours we vacuumed, dusted, mopped floors and cleaned windows. Christian was a multi-talented chef and his wife an interior designer. Their home was beautiful. Christian had done most of the renovations himself, converting this very old house into a lovely home, ensuring he retained its history. It was filled with antiques that had come from Lisette's ancestral family home in Paris. Grand, ornate portraits hung in pride of place. Enormous mahogany armoires stood against the walls. An antique writing desk, with all the little cubby holes filled with writing paper, ink and envelopes, sat under two large windows, facing the garden. Gilt mirrors, wonderful old couches and overstuffed armchairs in what looked to be old Sanderson floral fabrics completed the picture. So elegant.

Whacked at the end of all that cleaning, we sat for five minutes while Christian made us a reviving coffee. With cups in hand, he walked us through his very orderly, latticed-edged vegetable and herb garden. It was an absolute joy to behold. There was such a variety of lush and luxuriant herbs overflowing the borders. Christian was so very passionate about food that it was very easy to get caught up in his enthusiasm. The cherry, pear, walnut and other fruit trees in the orchard were prolific and he and Lisette spent days bottling and pickling. The larder shelves groaned with gourmet delights, ready to be savoured throughout the winter months and also to be given away as gifts. Lisette had given us large jars of bottled pears and pickled walnuts as a little extra thank you.

We may have slogged the afternoon away but it was wonderful to have had the pleasure of being in their old, French stone cottage. The main bathroom was the biggest room in the house. The bath, with its huge clawed feet and rolled top, had been cleverly centred in the room to take in the views through the two small, four-paned windows in opposite walls. It was situated to bring the outdoors in while luxuriating in a scent-filled, hot bath. There were two substantial, vitreous china pedestal basins, each different, very ornate and beautifully shaped. The mirrors above these were just as ornate, done in a gold filigree design. An antique, timbered side-table with a marble top sat alongside the bath. All manner of oils, candles, scrubs, scents and colognes were laid out. I loved this room the most. So beautiful and elegant after the shabby and cell-like bathrooms in the house we looked after. It truly wouldn't be overly expensive to transform ours. Just a matter of finding the right bits and pieces to add.

During the past week, we'd had other guests staying, as well as Philip and Peter. They all looked after themselves in the house kitchen, which meant no bother for me. However once they'd gone, the kitchen needed a good going-over again, from top to toe. We only had a few days until the boss arrived. I really wanted everything looking perfect for him in an attempt to win his approval and finally to prove we were competent and capable of running Mas de Lavande. Steve had finished checking every plug and light in the place to make sure they were working and I had every bed made up again, for the 'just in case' occasion. We'd learnt the hard way that guests could be sprung on us at a moment's notice.

The kittens finally came out of the wall. They were three adorable, fluffy bundles, rolling around on the gravel path. That was only until they spied a human. They would then high-tail it behind one of the storage boxes. This went on for a couple of days until we noticed one day there was only one kitten. Some large predator most likely got the other two. This last one was going to Siobhan and Doug's when we could catch it. Their children had already named it Kiwi.

The pressure mounted as the days raced on and the arrival time of the Cornwall Art Group drew ever closer. There were still finishing details to be sorted for the art studio. The pool filter had died and yet another man was due to arrive to replace this. It had been an intense time for everyone working there. The endless emailing of quotes, photographs and costings, plus discussions late into the evening with Sarah and/or Tristan, all added to the pressure. Steve had purchased two bottles of delicious red wine and several boxes of beers to give to the main building contractor. The men had been doing 12-hour days to complete to a deadline.

At long last the art studio and terrace were finished and the property was looking good. Two long trestle tables, bench seating and easels as well as soft furnishings had been purchased and delivered. A galley kitchen had also been installed with a huge, stainless steel sink in which to wash up brushes and other painting paraphernalia. Attractive shelving lined one wall to hold paint pots, water jars and brushes. It was going to be such a useful space.

The house was about to be filled to bursting with guests. It was time to start stocking up on all the necessities: toilet paper, bin bags and all the dry goods for the kitchen. Steve was fully occupied with the art studio and garden issues so I decided to take the bull by the horns and drive myself to the supermarket. I was determined to be independent but it was nerve-wracking to be in amongst a lot of traffic. I was hunched over the wheel and had to force myself to sit back in the seat and to breathe normally. Turning back into our driveway, I was thrilled to have finally done it for myself. It felt so good not waiting for, or relying on, Steve to drive me.

Everything was in hand so one morning we escaped the housework and garden and took ourselves into Toulouse. We had to collect Fifi La Trixi Belle anyway. After fumbling around on the newly fixed GPS, trying to find a landmark quickly in central Toulouse, we gave up and got ourselves lost.

'Let's just drive into the next parking area we come across,' I suggested to Steve. This happened to be the St George car park.

My heart gave a little skip as we came up the steps from the car park into the daylight. We found ourselves in a very smart, well-to-do part of Toulouse.

'Oooh, Steve, what a beautiful area,' I cooed at him, wide-eyed.

'Sure is! Very nice indeed,' he said, looking around.

I felt a little frisson of excitement. It was wonderful to be in the heart of gorgeous shops, cafés and outdoor restaurants after being in the countryside since we arrived.

My head was swivelling, taking in the sights and sounds. Men and women were immaculately groomed and coiffed. What a pleasure it was to be out amongst it all. I was rather surprised at my reaction and to think that I might actually miss that side of our life.

'I wonder if I can still fit into my high heels after all this time wearing my "flats",' I said to no one in particular, just voicing my thoughts. I would have to try them on to see. As I knew we were going into the city, I'd made an effort to dress a little better and had put on my white jeans, white singlet and a nice, red floral shirt. However, I was still in my flats as I didn't know how far we would be walking.

As we enjoyed our time away from our daily toil, we browsed through the different shops and found our way into the Place du Capitole. The Capitole is the heart of the municipal administration of Toulouse. It's 135 metres long, with the façade of the building dating from 1750 and built-in pink brick in a neoclassical design. It's an enormous and beautiful building. Toulouse is known as the pink city because of the brick colour. Many cafés lined the enormous square so we sat at one of these to enjoy our coffee and to watch Toulouse daily life unfold around us.

Back home we enjoyed yet another gorgeous, warm evening. In the shade outside our cottage, I set the rusty table for dinner. A small pork roast was in the oven (creating even more heat) with red onions, sage and the obligatory tiny French potatoes. I dry-fried slivered almonds and tossed these with blanched green beans, lemon juice, a little olive oil and seasoning. *Voilà*, another delicious al fresco meal. Those were the times I loved most, when we were on our own at Mas de Lavande and normally with a day's work behind us. Maggie Hatcher, Elle Macpherson, Hilda Ogden and Adele clucking around us and the cats curled up in the shade were our constant dinner companions and the drone and click of the cicadas our music. Utter bliss.

20

Open for Business

Tristan and his friend Penny had arrived the previous evening. The skies were azure blue, not a breath of wind, and it was so warm. As usual, the late Mr Rawson was *still* in the shower when they pulled up. I was the lone meeter and greeter but we left Steve to haul in the bags once he'd hurried up the path.

Everything 'looked lovely and welcoming' according to Penny. As she followed me to her room, she commented more than once on how fresh and clean it all looked. I knew Penny had often been to stay over the years so she made my day. Once out of the car and into their rooms, both were quick to change into something lighter. They were so hot in the jeans they'd been travelling in from London.

I'd laid the outside table with candles, flowers, crockery, cutlery and napkins. It all looked very pretty and welcoming. As an aperitif, I'd put together a small platter of olives, pork terrine from our market and my homemade cumin hummus with grilled ciabatta. A chilled bottle of Chablis sat in the ice bucket all ready to pour.

As requested, dinner was to be simple – roast chicken, salad of cos and curly lettuces, truss tomatoes, cucumber with lots of basil, parsley and chives and a vinaigrette dressing. That morning

I'd bought a free-range chicken from the market. Tristan and Penny were planning to cook for themselves but as their flight was delayed, I decided to get dinner underway. That way when they arrived they wouldn't have to worry about cooking. They could sit down with a glass of wine and just relax. As soon as the chicken was ready, I jointed it, wrapped it and the baby potatoes in foil to keep warm in the oven. 'Afters' were two local cheeses, dried apricots, fresh figs and almonds set on a small board, ready to nibble on. No dessert—as requested. Tristan was very weight-conscious.

They were both so pleased not to have to think about dinner. I felt we got the big tick from Tristan who, looking around, could see what we'd achieved. We hoped that laid the foundation for how we would now progress. Steve and I had worked so hard for so long to make it as perfect as we could, despite the previous niggles. Tristan did mention the next day a few things he didn't like and wanted changed but that was a learning curve for us. I didn't see this as a negative.

Early the next morning Steve went off to sort out the animals and did a run down to the bakery for me. I headed for the house to do the dishes and set up breakfast. The table under the large dining room window looked out over the valley and was a perfect place to eat breakfast. I set out muesli, yoghurts, cherries, sliced melon, peaches and nectarines plus a fresh baguette with pats of butter and my homemade strawberry jam. The food looked colourful and appetising. Penny's eyes lit up when she walked in.

'Oh, Annemarie! Yum, this looks perfect, thank you,' she said.

'You are very welcome, Penny. I hope you slept well. Coffee? Tea?' I offered, placing napkins on the side plates.

Tristan had been out for a run followed by a quick shower. There was no time for him to sit down to breakfast as he had an early meeting with Steve and one of the tradesmen. As he came through the door, with his hair still damp from the shower, I proffered a cup of coffee which he grabbed with both hands, a nod of the head to say thank you and headed out of the door.

Later that morning Steve and I sat down with Tristan to discuss forthcoming weeks and some of the property issues that required resolution. It was an excellent, productive meeting. He was delighted with how the artists' studio and terrace had turned out and at last we were up to speed with who was coming and when. Much easier to deal with just one person instead of two and to also be face to face and talk.

I drew up an Excel spreadsheet to keep track of nights and people. These arrangements could change at any time so we had to be ready. Sadly, Steve and I weren't involved in any discussions concerning arrangements for guests. We'd had great difficulty in getting responses re schedules and information which made it problematic to plan and prepare.

Late afternoon the heat outside was sending us all into a somnolent state. The buzzing and intermittent clicking of the cicadas was the only discernible noise to be heard. The temperature was so warm and sleep-inducing that Tristan and Penny had left their sun loungers for the comfort and cool of their semi-shuttered rooms. They'd opted for an hour's snooze before drinks and canapés. It was an all-enveloping blanket of heat. I, too, escaped for an hour to the cool of our room and closed my eyes as I sank into the bed.

21

Food, Glorious Food

I was cooking Tuesday night for Tristan, Penny and a small group of locals. The constant refrain was to keep it simple, use what was seasonal and, especially, use whatever was ready in the garden. Read this as spend as little as possible but make it fabulous! No pressure then. I'd bought pork fillets from a highly recommended local butcher. I'd stood in a queue which snaked out of the door and then I waited a good ten minutes to be served. Each customer was warmly greeted, their requirements discussed in detail as well as the cooking process involved. Their choice of meat cut was then meticulously and lovingly wrapped and handed to them with a very cheery *au revoir* and kind regards to the rest of the family.

I marinated the pork fillets in root ginger, garlic, mango chutney and a little olive oil. After it was cooked, I placed sliced rounds of the pork onto couscous tossed through with roasted peppers, courgettes, red onion, herbs and cherry tomatoes. Once plated, a topping of coriander leaves and pomegranate seeds completed the dish. A warm, pungent aroma wafted up from the pork fillets. A green bean salad was the accompaniment. French cheese followed while for dessert I'd made a walnut meringue topped with lemon curd and berries. I had a strawberry coulis ready, too, so used this as a base to sit the meringue on. Each course looked so appetising and colourful when I set down the plates in front of the guests. Tristan was a happy man and dinner was a success with everyone at the table.

We had a lot of organising to do, sorting out who was sleeping where during the Cornwall club stay and artists' workshops. The planning needed to ensure bedrooms were always ready for the next guests. We'd managed to enlist the help of a friend of a French woman we'd met. She was going to gather all the laundry during the two mornings of changes we would do for the large art club group and the artists' weeks. She would then take it to the laundromat, bring it back and press it. This would be a considerable saving of time and energy on my part and would leave me and one other to concentrate on the house, food, flowers and wine.

Steve had spent previous days up a ladder, fighting off wasps as he picked the last of the cherries. I'd bagged and frozen 13 kilos the previous week. Cherry jam would need to be on *my* list of chores, I thought. What a pain stoning them. For a bit of practice, I made a cherry pie and stoning four cups of the fruit took forever. The pie was a delicious mix of sweet, rich pastry filled with ruby-red, syrupy cherries. At some future date, it would be warmed through and eaten with runny cream. The aromas wafting out of the oven were so tantalising. Once the pie cooled, I wrapped it in cling film, put it into a freezer bag and popped it into the freezer. This pie would be an excellent fallback dessert should I ever need it.

22

Chocolate Terrine Receives
Rave Reviews

After a hectic week, Steve and I were relishing a night on our own. We were both exhausted and in need of quiet time. Tristan and Penny had gone to meet an art dealer somewhere further north and were staying overnight. A hot shower, dinner and wine had set my head in the nodding mode and I was struggling to stay awake. Back in New Zealand, I'm notorious for being in my PJs at an absurdly early hour during the winter. That particular summer night, I could be excused as I was shattered.

Saturday night's dinner was one to write up in my brag book. It was all thanks to the chef and mentor, Rebecca, who'd helped create an amazing chocolate terrine. Staying at Mas de Lavande and dining with Tristan were some high-flying London art collectors he'd met through his gallery business. They were on an extended French holiday and Tristan had invited them to stop off at the farmhouse for a couple of nights.

Our morning had been spent at the Albi market. Tristan had gone early to have coffee with a possible client so we met him at the front door of the covered market. He selected crunchy baby cos lettuce, courgettes, glossy aubergines, vine-ripened tomatoes and other fresh vegetables. I was chief cashier, handing over the money, and Steve was the bag man. He ferried everything to the car while Tristan and I went off to see his favourite fishmonger, Morin Marée, where we purchased a side of salmon, fresh oysters and marinated prawns. Morin Marée's store was a feast for the eyes. Gleaming fish and shellfish sat on ice and looked so fresh. Not a fly to be found under the counter glass. Our last stop was the chocolatier, Michel Belin.

It was so hard to choose as everything was beautifully presented and mouth-watering. The window display was a work of art, with delicious and colourful morsels displayed in pretty urns and boxes. We ended up with exquisite layered desserts in tiny glasses topped with little raspberries, strawberries or miniature chocolate shapes and gold shards. Other gourmet delights were slipped into the shopping basket.

'Right, Annemarie, Steve, would you mind going on ahead to get everything ready for lunch and store all this food in the chiller? I don't want anything going off in this heat,' Tristan asked. 'Heavens, look at the time,' he added, checking his watch. 'Our guests will be there in an hour. Can you give them a lovely welcome please if I'm not back in time? I should be there but just in case.'

'No, that's absolutely fine. Don't worry; we'll make sure everything is ready and will most definitely give your guests the best welcome,' I assured him. 'See you soon.' We waved and headed for our car.

Just as the last of the shopping was stored away, we heard the crunch of tyres on the gravel driveway and went out to welcome our special guests. They'd had a very stressful time getting from the airport to us and were so pleased to have arrived. Both were keen to get out of their sticky jeans, freshen up before lunch and slip into cooler clothing. Steve whisked their bags out of the boot and ushered them down to the *pigeonnier.* I popped the wine into a cooler and laid a tray with pâté, crackers, olives and nuts, adding glasses and napkins. I pulled some outdoor chairs into the shade where they could enjoy the stunning, long view down the lush, green valley. It was a clear blue sky and a beautiful day. As they came back up the path, Tristan arrived back to greet them, walking across the grass with them to sit down. They were so impressed with the place.

The following night after drinks and hors d'oeuvres on the art studio terrace, I served a dinner of baked salted salmon, the by-now compulsory baby potatoes in a little butter and herbs, green salad and layered basil, tomato and mozzarella salad. Nothing fancy, just simple, good food. Soft and hard blue and creamy cheeses came next. The magnificent chocolate terrine was the grand finale.

I was so stressed, knowing how vital it was to Tristan that everything was perfect. The day hadn't gone well for me. I'd given myself an electric shock on one of the lamps, walked into the electrical wire surrounding the kitchen garden, banged my shoulder hard on a low shelf and burnt myself on the oven. What else could possibly happen?

As I was taking the raw salmon from the fridge, it slid off the plate and onto the ingrained-dirt, rough-cast stone floor. It fell partly onto my sandalled foot but mostly on the floor. Oh. My. God! That's what could go wrong. I was almost out of control with nerves. I scooped that fish up, quickly washed it and patted it dry, hoping like hell it was thoroughly clean. While I was flapping about, one of the cats had snuck in the kitchen door. With his raspy tongue, he was in raptures, licking my foot and sandal.

I could hear chatter in the dining room so I knew that everyone was in, ready for dinner. I was in such a lather (heat in the kitchen, menopause and stress). Steve followed me out to the dining room, carrying the plated cooked salmon to the serving table. I didn't trust myself to keep it on the platter. It was to be a self-service buffet but right then and there Tristan decided it would be easier if I plated the salmon for everyone. They could then help themselves to the rest. The only light came from candles on the table and some low lighting from the wall lamps. Steve was standing beside me, holding the plates while I sliced the salmon. Thank heavens we had our backs to everyone seated as I looked in horror at the salmon pieces. I screeched at him in a whisper (if that's possible), 'I don't think the salmon is properly cooked!'

It was so hard to tell really, due to the poor lighting. Steve whispered back, 'Everyone has sat down; it's too late. You just have to serve it.'

I felt sick to my stomach and my heart was pounding. All I could think was how vital it was for Steve and me to get everything right. I desperately wanted it all to be perfect for Tristan. We passed the salad platters around, making sure everyone had what they needed, and then disappeared into the kitchen.

Falling back against the closed kitchen door, I was close to tears and almost hysterical. I moaned to Steve, 'That's it. I've blown it.'

He just rolled his eyes. 'Buck up,' he said. 'There's a lot more to do.'

We both set to, cleaning up. No further words were spoken between us as we prepared the cheese boards and set out the dessert plates. I was an absolute misery after my day of mishaps and the accumulated stress of previous events. It came time to clear the main plates.

'I can't bear to look at anyone. I'm going to slink in and slink out,' I muttered to Steve.

Well, what a shock and such an unexpected reaction.

'Wow, that salmon was absolutely delicious.'

'It was perfect.'

'I loved that.'

All these lovely comments hailed from different places around the table. I couldn't believe it. What looked undercooked in that dim light must have been just right. My relief was enormous and I couldn't stop beaming.

With the cheese course out of the way, I would have liked to pipe the chocolate terrine into the dining room, just like the

Scots do with haggis. It looked like a culinary masterpiece, sitting on a white piece of marble, surrounded by luscious raspberries and strawberries. A jug of strawberry coulis completed the picture. It was certainly the pièce de résistance. Thank heavens for Rebecca and her fabulous skills. I knew it would be a success.

As I cleared the dessert plates, there was almost a standing ovation. Everyone was in raptures over the terrine. Woohoo!

After a final wipe down of the kitchen benches and hobs, a quick scan of the room to ensure everything was in order, I flicked off the lights. Steve and I put our heads around the kitchen door to say goodnight. Tristan followed us out.

'Annemarie, that was a sensational dinner. Thank you both very much. The evening went very well.'

Tristan then kissed me on the cheek and said goodnight. Wow! That was such a wonderful gesture and truly gladdened my heart. I slept well that night.

23

Exploring

It was Wednesday and at last it was a full day off. Hurray! We'd had to negotiate this time off with Sarah but were still given work instructions. Before we could leave, I had to ensure the kitchen was cleaned up from the previous evening and lay out breakfast. It was only Tristan and Penny staying and Tristan could be very hands-on when he wanted. Steve had to make sure the chickens were fed, the pool sorted and the garden watered which meant being up early again. No lie-in on our day off. It was after 9 a.m. before we ducked and dived our way to the car, trying not to be seen. We didn't want to answer questions or be asked to do something else before we could leave. We did it! I exhaled heavily as we went down the drive, thankful we'd escaped.

First stop was Cahors, the principal city of the Lot Department which sits right on a bend of the meandering River Lot. It's a bustling tourist town, with its main attractions being the medieval quarter and the 14th-century fortified Valentré Bridge. We had a great explore around the town and enjoyed a takeaway lunch as we sat on one of the many park benches dotted around. The Middle Eastern pita bread, stuffed with salad, hummus and shaved lamb was delicious. I just had to have a browse through the very elegant antique shop in the main street and enjoyed looking at all the beautiful, old French pieces. The owner sat outside in one of the old armchairs he was selling, enjoying his cigarette and chatting with the locals as they went about their daily business.

Window boxes were a riot of reds, pinks and white, sitting against cream stone buildings. Verdant parks were dotted throughout and old, black, ornate lamps all contributed to Cahors' prettiness. The setting was completed by beautiful views out over the sparkling river far below. Several hours later we were back in the car and, according to Google, driving on to 'one of the most beautiful villages in France', Saint-Cirq-Lapopie. It truly was. The village perched on the cliff face, 100 m above the river. The location was purposely chosen for its defensive position. It was hard to comprehend how the village hadn't slipped into the flowing water below over the centuries.

We drove and drove. Both of us loved the sense of freedom while out exploring and not working, oohing and aahing at all we saw. It felt like a real holiday outing. Hours flew by while we meandered through the villages and towns of Puylaroque, Caussade and Montricoux. As we stopped for a very welcome cold drink and coffee in an air-conditioned inn, it was a relief to be cool again, even for a brief time. It was 40 degrees that day and driving in a car with no air conditioning was awful, even with all the windows down. By the time we returned to the cottage, our clothes and hair were stuck to us, and our faces red, wet and shiny. The cool water of the shower had never felt so good as we freshened up and stepped into clean clothes. A quick bite to eat and we were off again to Doug and Siobhan's for a drink before heading to one of the music evenings in the bar in one of the local villages.

Doug and Siobhan were such great, welcoming, fun people. We always looked forward to our visits with them. After an hour or so chatting and laughing at the garden table, listening to the kids shouting and squealing on the trampoline, Steve and I climbed back into the car and drove on to the pub. At the entrance to the bar, a narrow stairway led down to a very small room below. Everyone squashed in here to listen to anyone that wanted to sing and/or play an instrument. A few locals attended but most of the people were English with some French and the occasional Dutch and Belgian. Everyone sang along. Sadly that was the last music evening until the end of September when they would resume again. We'd discovered these music evenings after we'd chatted with an English couple we met in the supermarket. They were there that evening and once they recognised us beckoned us over. They invited us to their place for an aperitif and we hoped to go when we had another day off.

We had quite a few other guests stay after Tristan and Penny. They were all friends or acquaintances of Tristan and Richard and came from all parts of the world and at varying times. Part of our brief was to offer to make guests' beds and clean their bathrooms every morning. Most people said not to bother but those that did want that service were gracious and thankful. The majority of the guests were interesting and very nice and friendly with us so we enjoyed them. All were intrigued that we were New Zealanders, exclaiming what a fabulous place our home country is. Always they asked what we were doing on that side of the world.

In between guests Tristan came back to stay on his own for a few days. I added personal assistant to my job description during this visit as I scurried along behind him on a tour of the house, taking notes and measurements and emailing these off to all and sundry. New items were ordered for the main house and the *pigeonnier*. I did wonder when we would get the new furnishings and furniture he'd promised. We'd emailed our meagre list through but still no word.

Everything appeared to be going well now; at least, from our perspective it was. Earlier niggles seemed to have been forgotten and right then life was on an even keel. We'd put in some big days and weeks preceding and in between all the visitors. We were tired but satisfied and rather proud we had the place looking its best. What had been so very encouraging were the compliments and thank yous we'd received from the guests.

Some nights when people were staying, we got in our cottage door after 11 p.m., had a cup of tea and fell into bed. We dreaded the alarm going off at 6 a.m., or earlier if Steve had to do an airport run.

24

Humiliation

The day drew closer and closer for the Cornwall Art Club group to arrive and I was mindful that Steve and I would need to schedule a day trip to IKEA to buy all we needed. Once we got the go-ahead, that is. With no response about either the lists or the handbook, I went in search of Tristan. He was staying a few days with two old Richmond wine club friends. I had my lists and handbook tucked under my arm.

Tristan was at the dining table on his laptop while the friends sat on the sofas, reading or dozing. I excused myself, explained why I was there and asked if we could meet later in the afternoon to discuss everything.

'No, no, let's do it now,' he said, flapping his hands at me, indicating I should sit down.

'Should we go into the office?' I asked.

'No, no, here is fine,' he curtly replied.

It felt a little awkward having to go through everything in front of his friends but I needed answers so I began.

Tristan didn't even look at me or the lists and appeared very distracted. He carried on jabbing away at his laptop. It was obviously not a good time and I didn't want to bother him so again I offered to come back later.

'No, show me that list now!' he snapped. The two friends, who couldn't help but hear, looked up.

It was so embarrassing. Finally he turned from his laptop. As his eyes started to scan through everything, he turned on me. 'How much money do you think I have, Annemarie? We don't need all this glassware. Look in the cupboard; there's plenty,' he said shrilly.

Tristan pushed his chair back, stood up and threw open the cupboard where I'd hidden all the clutter. Here was the mish-mash of glassware. All were different sizes, colours and shapes and some were chipped. Tristan began pulling everything out. Drawing his friends into the debacle, he spouted, 'These are perfectly adequate, don't you think?'

Well, what were they going to say? They were enjoying a nice little freebie in a beautiful part of France. From Tristan's intimation when he'd been there on his own, they didn't bother staying in touch for the rest of the year. One of the friends looked at me with a smug smirk. Next to be condemned, with a snort of derision, were the pâté and cheese knives plus the decent salad servers I'd dared put on the list.

'This is a French country farmhouse, not an English drawing room, for God's sake! We don't need all those silly things. You can take those off the list.'

I felt my face redden.

Why on earth did he ask me to make a list of what I thought we needed if he had no intention of changing or improving anything? These were the sorts of things I had at home; didn't he in Richmond? Tristan continually changed his mind. His requests had led to hours of fruitless research, phone calls and hard work, on both Steve's and my part. That afternoon deteriorated even further.

By now my face was flaming. I felt so humiliated in front of his friends, both watching and listening. I could tell one in particular was enjoying my discomfort. I stood up.

'Maybe it would be better if we finished this at a later time,'

I mumbled, gathering all my papers together and trying to make a dignified exit. Well, Tristan wouldn't stop.

'There won't be another time. I've already told you what's necessary and not necessary. Everything here is perfectly functional. I'm not made of money, Annemarie. End of story,' ranted Tristan.

Thank God I got through the door before the tears started. I hurried down the path to our cottage and to Steve, blubbing my eyes out and feeling like a chastised scullery maid. Steve put his arm around my shoulders, trying to comfort me as I explained my tears.

'You should have known what would happen. Try and let it go,' he soothed.

I needed to grow a thicker skin if I was to cope. My heart was hardening and I was re-evaluating exactly how much effort I would go to from then on.

The next morning it was as if nothing had happened. Tristan was all sweetness and light. I wasn't. I was angry and it was obviously written all over my face. Tristan inquired what the problem was so I told him, politely but firmly. It felt good to stand up to him. I don't think he was used to that. Sadly he just shrugged and turned his back, dismissing me and the incident. Having sorted breakfast I left the house and waited until the coast was clear for me to return to tidy up.

During our journey to IKEA to collect items already approved, Steve and I talked about the incident and other unwelcome news we'd been given.

'I don't know how much more I can cope with, Steve. Especially after Sarah's phone call telling me I don't know how to clean a bathroom or tidy a bedroom,' I said.

'Yes, that was ridiculous. I helped you with the room. It was perfectly clean,' he replied.

'Well, it's that and then the instruction I was to pick up Tristan's clothes, hang them up for him and do his laundry. That was never mentioned during our calls or while we were in London and certainly wasn't on the job description.' I moaned.

'I think Tristan and Sarah are making things up as they go along,' Steve said.

After my initial shock and offence, I endeavoured to be gracious and get on with it. I didn't realise that I was to be a personal maid as well as everything else. And please! Clean a bathroom? I really didn't understand what the issues were. I have high standards and pride myself on doing a good job. I found Sarah's comments (and delivery) very distressing. She was so rude and snippy and I took it all so personally. I wondered why Tristan never addressed any of those things with me directly. I was only ever down the path or in another room in the house.

With jangled nerves after standing up to Tristan, it was a relief to leave the place and be en route to IKEA. While we were walking through the aisles, the mobile rang. Guess who?

'Tristan here, Annemarie darling. I think we need to replace some of the glassware. Could you please pick up a dozen water glasses and a dozen red wine glasses while you're there?'

I couldn't believe my ears. I must have given some sort of response and as I hit the 'end' button I spun round to Steve and said, 'You won't believe this!'

I couldn't wait for Tristan and his friends to leave. We could then get back to enjoying being just us, living and working in the beautiful countryside with the animals, the lovely people we got to work with and our new-found friends.

25

Our Week with the Cornwall Art Club

What a week it had been! Bruce had come to work with us for the week while the art group were there and the three of us were shattered but elated. It had gone so well. Steve had dropped him back to the airport on the last day after many hugs and kisses and thank yous from our guests.

Bruce had arrived the previous Friday, having flown in from Marbella. What an absolute godsend. He was a Londoner and an old friend of Tristan's, now living in Marbella with his boyfriend and working part-time in a café there. He was fabulous at laying a beautiful table, throwing together an inviting salad or arranging a stunning posy of wildflowers from the house garden and he worked hard. Sometimes for afternoon tea, he would produce a magnificent cake or scones with cream and jam, all of which our art lovers oohed and aahed over. Bruce was good fun too. The three of us got on extremely well and we felt we produced a fantastic week for our guests.

We had no idea how much we'd spent on food as I hadn't entered all the receipts into the spreadsheet. I was a little concerned we would be in trouble once the bank statements came through. By the end of that wonderful week, though, I was over my constant worrying whether everything was OK. The brief had been to give them a week to remember and I know we did that—very successfully.

Even though each person appeared comfortably off, they were all grounded, very relaxed and easy to get on with. The organiser requested a pizza night for one of the dinners and we brought these in from a local pizzeria. They asked us to join them and have a glass of wine so we were able to chat and relax a bit. Other than the pizza night and one night when they all went off to a local gourmet market, we cooked the entire week. It was very late before Steve, Bruce and I sat down to eat at our little cottage table (in the dark, but a lovely cool temperature). Our dinner would be whatever we'd made for the guests, always making extra for ourselves. We'd then fall into bed around midnight. The alarm was set for 6.00 a.m. when I would dash through the shower and get over to the house. After-dinner wine glasses needed to be washed, dishwashers emptied and the table laid ready for breakfast. First task was always flicking on the coffee machine and the kettle for the early risers.

While I was working in the kitchen, Steve would tend to the animals. In the pool area, he'd reset the outdoor furniture, sweep up leaves, clean the pool and place fresh towels on the loungers. Next on his list would be the long, slow process of watering the kitchen garden and ornamental beds. Steve had suggested to Tristan that he and Gabriel could easily put in a watering system. The hosing wouldn't be that expensive but the answer had been a resounding 'no'. Bruce stayed at the B&B down the road and would stop at the bakery every morning on his way to us. He smelt delicious and mouth-watering when he came through the kitchen door, his arms full of freshly baked baguettes and bags of plain and chocolate croissants. Once everything was laid out the three of us would return to our cottage to have breakfast together. Bruce was always smiling and happy to muck in, making for a smooth and relaxed working relationship.

Breakfast was from 8 a.m. until 10 a.m. but it wasn't an issue if someone wanted a lie-in and to eat something mid-morning. Everyone was very laid-back and always considerate towards us. After coffee-making and loading dishwashers, Bruce and I would slip upstairs to remake beds, open curtains and windows while the artists were either out for a walk or at breakfast. We'd do a quick sluice around hand basins, showers and toilets, making sure everything was fresh and clean. The dishwashers were going three times a day and we were forever cleaning up. The week was hard work but we enjoyed our guests. They created such a comfortable atmosphere, we felt like we were hosting friends, rather than serving strangers.

After breakfast the art group would break into smaller groups. Some would go off exploring; some would work in the art studio and others would set up their easels in a quiet place on the property and spend a few hours creating landscapes.

One evening we planned an informal barbecue and set up three trestle tables under the huge plane trees at the top of a knoll in the garden. Steve had lit the barbecue an hour earlier to have it ready to cook the prepared vegetables and meat. Nestled amongst the embers, potatoes were roasting in tin foil. These were going to be delicious with salt and creamy Normandy butter melting into them.

Bruce and I hiked between the kitchen and the tables with platters of food we'd put together: green salads with lots of herbs; roasted beetroot, feta and walnut salad and a huge platter of sliced tomatoes layered with rounds of goats' cheese and fresh basil scattered over the top. Bruce had whisked up a jug of balsamic dressing for all the salads.

The table looked so inviting. Candles flickered in the large hurricane lamps, and colourful salads, checked napkins, glassware and cutlery made it such a country affair. Our guests were delighted with it all. It was a beautiful evening with a soft breeze and few pestiferous insects. That breeze was very welcome after an extremely hot day. With a glass of wine in hand, platters of cheese nearby, everyone sat back, chatted and watched the moon come up. A perfect end to a perfect day.

The temperatures had been up to 44°C at times. Thank goodness we were having a breather and it had dropped down to low-30s. At night all we needed was a sheet to cover us and not even that sometimes. The fan whirred the whole night, trying to keep the air circulating. So often we showered twice, three times a day to cool off. If we were alone at the property, we'd fall into the pool before bed.

Before our lovely group arrived, I'd hit rock bottom. I was finding it difficult to be positive and was too miserable to sit and write in my online diary. Those earlier, upsetting situations we had to deal with had thrown me. I was getting concerned emails and messages from friends asking were we OK as there'd been nothing on my blog for a good few weeks.

However, our time with the art club boosted me no end. At the end of that week, we were on a high. We knew we were doing a good job. The comments and feedback and the enormous tip we'd received confirmed this. They weren't alone with their praise. Others who'd stayed had been very complimentary. I didn't know what more we could have done.

In hindsight Steve and I did wonder how many issues may have been initiated or exaggerated by Sarah. This was the first time Tristan and Richard had engaged an agent. She was a very different person in front of Tristan than she was with us. I'd noticed any snipes or comments were never by email, always verbal. So we had no record, should the need arise.

Tristan on the other hand appeared not to like how well we got on with those that visited Mas de Lavande—guests *and* tradespeople. I think I was the problem at that stage. Steve seemed to be receiving the better end of the stick. That was until Steve complained to Sarah about the flooring contractor during the studio construction.

The phone had rung.

'It's Sarah,' Steve said, looking up from the phone at me.

'Now what?' I muttered to him.

'Sarah, hi,' said Steve as he hit the green button.

'Hello, Steve. Tristan was asking what's happening with the flooring in the art studio. It seems to be taking an inordinate amount of time,' she said.

'Well, it would be done by now if the contractor didn't stuff up all the time. Firstly he arrived with the wrong floorboards and had to return to Albi to re-order the right ones. That took a week. When he finally arrived with the correct boards, he miscalculated how many nails and screws he needed and had to make a trip to Brico Dépôt to buy more. Then he ran out of stain a few days later and had to order more. He's been so disorganised. In hindsight, Tristan should never have accepted his quote,' Steve told her.

'I beg your pardon? How incredibly rude of you. He's an excellent tradesman. For your information he's a family friend of my parents and has done a lot of this work over the years,' Sarah retorted.

Steve shrugged. 'Sorry, Sarah, but it's the truth. That's why it's all taken so long,' he responded. 'It's been difficult, to say the least. He said he'd be finished tomorrow. I'll send you some photos.'

The conversation ended there, with polite goodbyes from both sides.

26

Other Opportunities

As I was so unhappy, I'd been looking around at what other employment might be available to us. We asked for, and got, two days off in a row in between bookings and drove through to the French department of Gers. Here we met with a couple who ran a property management business. They would open and close French holiday homes for UK owners and take care of any security and maintenance issues when the owners were absent. There was also the option of cooking for the owners. This trip to see them proved very interesting and thought-provoking.

Steve and I spent three hours discussing with them how it all worked. Their house was being sold with the business. This was something we needed to be very sure of. Steve and I thrashed it through as much as we could while driving. We needed to sit down with pen and paper and work out whether it would be financially viable for us to take on the business and the house.

A few days later, it was with a huge sigh of relief that Steve did another airport run and we waved goodbye to our boss as he headed back to London. During his visits we would sometimes get a text message from Siobhan and Doug, saying,

Dinner at ours tonight. Check if you're needed at the house.

If not, come to us. Doesn't matter what time; just get here when you can. Let us know.

They were so thoughtful and kind. Instead, with Tristan gone, we took the opportunity to invite Siobhan, Doug and the kids over to us for a swim and a BBQ one afternoon. We'd been at their place so often, it was great to offer them hospitality.

Gabriel called asking us to join them at a local gourmet market with his family that same evening. They knew Siobhan and Doug, too, so it wasn't a problem to take them along with us. After a swim we set off in convoy, following Gabriel through the narrow village streets.

What a wonderful community event the night market was, held in a tiny village not far from us.

For 3€ you could hire a plate, knife, fork and glass and once returned at the end of the evening, you received a refund of 1.50€. What a great concept. You took your plate to the various stalls, made your choice from meaty, savoury sausage, pungent local cheese or sizzling pork chops. Fragrant, alluring smoke from the many barbecues wafted past, making us salivate. Also available was *aligot*, the famous creamy potato dish, full of Cantal cheese and crème fraîche. We could turn our plates upside down and it wouldn't fall off. Everyone either sat on hay bales, squashed together randomly at long trestle tables or on fold-up chairs. It was a wonderful time for those catching up with old friends and family. CD music blared out of speakers set up at various points and children careered around, shrieking and dancing.

Siobhan and Doug were well equipped and had brought plates, knives and forks and plastic glasses with them for us all. They'd done this before. The longest queues were for the fries and ice cream. It was a great evening but all too soon it was time to leave. I nodded off in the car after one too many red wines. As soon as we arrived home, I fell into bed. It was a wonderful feeling, knowing it was just us again at Mas de Lavande with no complications for a while.

Steve managed to get away to see a stage of the Tour de France. After weeks of planning (and a recce on the way home from Gers), he installed himself on an upward grind for the cyclists, in a place called La Française. Steve used to commute by bike and is a keen cyclist. He was very excited as he'd been captivated by the annual TV commentary and this was his first time seeing part of the Tour de France live. Our brother-in-law John had emailed to get Steve's exact bearings, in the hope that he would see him on TV. John is an avid cyclist, too. He and my sister Adrienne had followed the Tour de France by car on one of their European trips.

Steve parked the car, slung his small backpack on his shoulder and walked for about three kilometres. He set up his New Zealand and All Black flags and stood chatting excitedly with other cycling fans patiently waiting on the roadside. The sponsors came through first with music blaring from the speakers on their vans as they threw branded merchandise into the crowds. Forty-five minutes later, the support crews and then the leaders, closely followed by the peloton, arrived in a blinding flash of colour, spokes and tanned legs. Hold your breath! They all disappeared at break-neck speed around the corner. It was all done and dusted in less than five minutes. Steve then turned and walked the three kilometres back to the car and came home. It was such a massive build-up for such a short time but he just loved his live experience. John never did see him on the telly. The only cycling Steve managed to fit in was up to our *tabac* to get the bread.

When Gabriel and Suzanne went on holiday, we had the pleasure of hosting their chickens for their very own holiday. Gabriel brought them round in a crate and released them into the chook house with ours. Talk about ruffled feathers. Maggie Hatcher was most indignant and tried to peck the unwelcome visitors. Hilda Ogden probably worried they might get more food than her and Elle Macpherson kept walking around them just to make sure no one was more beautiful than her. As for Adele, she continued to belt out the squawks. It was a major stand-off in the coop. Our girls weren't happy having three strangers visiting. After a couple of hours, however, they settled down and it wasn't long before they were all out together, pecking around the gardens and following Steve around the property.

27

The Artists' Workshop Week

During the Cornwall Art Club stay, every bed was occupied and every room in the house used. As a consequence it had taken three long days to get Mas de Lavande back in order. Each bed was stripped back to the mattress and all the linen washed at either the laundromat or in the house washing machines. Then there was the ironing.

We had, unfortunately, been let down by the girl who was to have helped me with all the laundry. I ended up doing two runs to the local laundromat midweek, using all their three machines. It was the same process at the end of the week. The resultant piles of sheets and towels were enormous. The guests had used every towel and pool towel, as well as all the bathrobes. Next was the house cleaning. Luckily Siobhan came in to help for a day. That broke the back of it, and damaged mine!

Once the house was back to a clean state, I began titivating the rooms to get ready for the artists. Checklist: a fresh robe, fresh towels with lavender sprigs, hand towels and face cloths. Tick. I'd replaced and refilled the soaps and shower gels in the bathrooms. Tick. Water bottles sat at each bedside and vases stood waiting for flowers on the day of their arrival. Tick. The place looked immaculate and we were ready for the next wave of guests.

That night we received an upsetting email. Steve and I wouldn't be required for the two middle days of the two workshops.

Together, Tristan and Sarah concocted a story about us needing some relaxation time. From the wording, Steve and I knew it was about saving money but, still, we were to be around the property should we be needed by guests or them. What on earth was going on? None of it made sense as this would be such a busy time. These two weeks would also have earned us some extra money, as had been promised at the start of this job. Why were they doing this to us? This was the final straw. We felt so used and abused. That was when it truly hit home that we were a disposable item—skivvies for the summer letting period. There was certainly none of the expected property management or business-building involved.

We voiced our disagreement with this manipulative and mean proposal, received a verbal apology and the email was withdrawn. Again I was supposed just to accept these situations and move on. I found that such a difficult thing to do.

We then found out that for these artists' weeks, Tristan had engaged family friends of Richard's to come and cook. This was (presumably) the driver for the attempt to cut our pay. The cook had brought his wife along with him to help with all the prep work. Together they would do lunch and dinner, leaving me to sort out the buffet breakfast and the rest of the house. Brilliant. I was pleased with that arrangement as it would have been a Herculean task to do it all myself.

Sarah had enlisted the help of a young man called Harry to come and work with me to take care of the house. The story went that Harry had received appalling A level results and his parents were furious. They were making him do various courses to find which path his life should take. Currently he was doing a hospitality course and working in a private boutique hotel part-time in London to earn some money. He was being given all the menial jobs and wasn't happy.

The art tutor for the two separate weeks would be Shelley. She had a reputation for being one of the best tutors in London and was a true professional. Well, with everyone on board and committed, I knew the week would be a fabulous one. It had worked brilliantly with the Cornwall Art Club.

Tristan would also be with us, ostensibly hosting the week. It wasn't only going to be about the art lessons. Incorporated into the week were visits to local markets, galleries, food and wine tastings, soaking up the culture of France and enjoying a little country life along the way. There were a lot of such weeks available throughout the greater area and all over France.

The rest of the house team arrived at Mas de Lavande two days before the budding artists and Tristan. I really liked Shelley. I was sure she would be a hit with all her pupils and it was so good to have another female around. Harry appeared a nice lad, if a little sullen and a bit prima donna-ish. None of his current issues were his fault, according to him. The husband and wife cooking team were good fun. That night they were trialling a couple of their recipes on us and we were all happy to be their guinea pigs. Harry loosened up and we had fun bonding and getting to know each other, sharing some wine and great food. I began to relax and had the feeling we were going to be a great team. Harry regaled us with stories about Tristan, whom his parents had known for a few years. Most of these stories were less than complimentary and some quite derogatory. Harry had only come because his parents thought he could do with the experience and because Sarah had asked him to help out and he'd never been to France before.

Together we (the house team) had put a rough plan in place how the week would proceed. I would be the early bird as I was on site. My job would be emptying dishwashers and reloading them with coffee cups and glasses from the night before. Next would be laying out the breakfast and making coffees and tea for any early risers. Steve would go off to get the bread and pastries and see to the animals, the garden and pool. While guests were at breakfast, Harry would arrive from the B&B. He and I were to make beds, open windows and do a quick clean of the bathrooms. Back in the dining room, together we would clear the breakfast things and leave the kitchen clean, ready for the cook and his wife to prepare lunch.

Harry and I would serve the lunch and help with the clean-up. As the early morning start was part of my duties, the after-dinner clean-up would be Harry's. Both of us would also do whatever was necessary during the day. A few hours off in the afternoon would give us a chance to put our feet up before it was time to set up for canapés and dinner. All sounded fair and manageable.

Little did I realise how it would all turn out. I'd been rather naïve, taking everyone at face value, thinking they were as open and honest as I was—what a fool. In hindsight this was a ridiculous notion on my part.

Our first full day of the artists' workshop had begun. Guests had started arriving the previous afternoon from about 4 p.m. Some drove to Mas de Lavande and others flew into Toulouse Airport where Steve collected them. Everyone jumped out of the vehicles, very excited to be there and exclaimed how pretty the house was. The day had turned from an overcast sky to brilliant afternoon sunshine. The house basked in the sunlight. Tristan and our crew went out to meet the guests.

The air was full of noisy chatter as hellos and kisses were exchanged and introductions made.

Tristan looked down at his checklist.

'OK, everyone, can I have your attention please? Annemarie and Steve will take you to your rooms. If you just listen for your names and which rooms you're in, you can then follow Annemarie and Steve. Thank you.'

Steve and I grabbed bags from the vehicles and with guests in tow took these upstairs to their various rooms in the house and to the *pigeonnier*. Once settled in, everyone met on the terrace for drinks and our first evening of the art course began. A very busy week was ahead of us and it had proved to be a hectic day already. We needed to empty dishwashers and set the table with flowers, candles and silver cutlery. We got started so all would be gleaming and beautiful for our guests.

The cooks had prepared a delicious first dinner of barbecued chicken, beef and vegetarian kebabs; orzo and basil pesto salad; green salad and tomato, cucumber, red onion and watermelon salad. Dessert was apricot tarte tatin with runny cream.

Harry and I went back and forth to the table with platters of food and plates and then returned to clear the empty dishes. This informal and relaxed dinner gave the pupils a chance to get to know each other and for Shelley to introduce her various techniques. The wine was flowing. Tristan was looking a little glazed and getting loud. I heard him make several inappropriate interpretations of Shelley's technique explanations. Shelley wasn't amused. There were polite titters from the guests but also several raised eyebrows around the table. Unfortunately he was making a bit of a fool of himself. Shelley was supposed to be the centre of attention, not him.

28

We are Leaving

What a shambles it turned out to be. The artists' workshop week started so well and ended up so awful for Steve and me. By the second day, Harry had shown his true colours. Somehow he just couldn't get out of bed and arrive on time to help me with beds and bathrooms and clearing up after breakfast. Funnily enough he did manage to get there in time to help himself to a coffee and a lovely chit-chat with the guests. I was getting so cross. If he wasn't talking with them, he'd become bosom buddies with the cook and his wife. Harry spent a lot of time in the kitchen, allegedly helping them. He'd been employed to help *me*. I was run ragged. It was such a difficult situation as Harry was the son of Sarah's friends and well known to Tristan.

'Harry, listen. I really need you to work with me. I can't do all this on my own and have the rooms ready for the guests and the kitchen clean for cook to prepare lunch,' I said.

Harry just laughed and flounced off towards the kitchen, calling over his shoulder, 'Oh, Annemarie, it'll be fine. Don't stress. I'll catch up with you upstairs. You're so bossy,' he smirked.

Undoubtedly true! Nothing changed. I was so annoyed at how selfish and lazy he was. What possessed Sarah to have Harry come and help? He was only interested in having fun. That might explain why he'd bombed out in his A levels.

It all turned to custard several mornings later. I was in the kitchen clearing the breakfast mess when Steve came in to get a drink. He was facing me and glanced at the clock on the wall.

'Still no sign of Harry then? His behaviour is just not good enough,' he said. 'He's always arriving late, leaving so much of the work to you. He's so damn lazy.'

Oh my god! Guess who had finally arrived? Harry was standing right behind Steve, unbeknown to him. Hearing all that was said, Harry's face crumpled. He stormed off in search of Tristan. Unfortunately it was the truth; something Harry didn't want to hear. I hoped Tristan would put him straight and Harry would start to pull his weight.

Nothing was said to us about the incident but there was a definite chill in the air. From then on Harry was allowed to carry on as he had been, arriving late and helping me, begrudgingly, and only when I pushed for him to do something. How I wished I had the nerve to tell Tristan precisely what Harry had said about him. However, I refused to stoop to their level. All this angst was very tiresome and stressful with a house full of guests. It wasn't easy putting on a smile, trying to be civil and look as though we were a team.

Thank goodness the guests were a great bunch. Steve and I got to enjoy them and have a bit of a chat as we worked. They would wander out to the garden and chat with him or with me as I was working my way around the house. It was a pleasure to wheel out trays of tea, coffee and cake in the afternoon to keep them going until dinner. The lovely couple in the *pigeonnier* kept asking me to have a cuppa with them.

'Annemarie, stop for a minute. Come and sit down and chat with us,' the woman said.

'Do you know, I would really love that but it just isn't possible right now. I would be in big trouble if I were caught. Maybe we could have a chat after dinner tonight? I'm keen to hear all about Cornwall. It's one place I'd love to see,' I said. We agreed to meet later that evening.

The workload was pretty intense. Part of this was a midweek linen change. This meant full sets of sheets and pillowcases, bathroom towels and pool towels. All the dirty linen needed to be taken down to the laundry and beds and bathrooms made up with fresh linen and towels. Two bedrooms were on the same floor, one on the ground floor with three on the upper. There was also the *pigeonnier* to sort out. The laundry was an open area inside the back door and, unfortunately, there was no space to iron. That was a real problem. When the house was full, our small living space at the cottage had stacks of linen waiting for me to iron it.

With that morning's chores completed, I took myself off to the local laundromat. The washing machines were huge and I filled the three of them with the basket loads I'd squeezed into the back of the car. I spent three hours loading in the sheets and towels then pulling them out and piling them into the dryers. I stood folding it all once it had finished drying. Thank goodness the guests had gone out for the morning. That gave me much-needed time to get through the laundry before they returned to Mas de Lavande for a late lunch. I thought, rather callously, *Oh well, Harry's there. He can set everything up for a change.* It had been such a relief to escape the tension in the house.

I was physically tired, mentally worn down and utterly miserable. I felt we were being unnecessarily ostracised for what had happened in the kitchen several days ago. Also the ugly email we'd received, wanting to cut our hours, was still on my mind. There I sat in the laundromat, snivelling into my tissues, wondering how on earth it had all got this bad.

Returning to the farmhouse, I pulled up on the driveway. As I hauled out the first basket of laundry, I could see Harry standing in the doorway, hands on hips. He yelled out to me, 'Annemarie, where on earth have you been? Everyone is due back in 20 minutes and the dining room needs vacuuming.'

Unbelievable. I wanted to slap him. Instead I think I stood there with a gaping mouth, staring at him. I couldn't believe what I was hearing from this self-centred 19-year-old. Steve, coming up the path, heard what Harry said and went ballistic.

'Who the hell do you think you are, talking to Annemarie like that? All morning she's been doing mountains of laundry. What have you been doing? I saw you through the window, standing there chatting in the kitchen. Go and do it yourself, you lazy fool.' He was at the end of his tether, too.

Well, that was the nail in our coffin. We know Harry complained (again) to Tristan and found out he'd emailed Sarah but I was beyond caring.

That same disastrous day, the very lovely couple staying in the *pigeonnier* announced they were getting married. They were older and on their second time around. He'd taken her off into Albi for a restaurant lunch and in the gardens of the Berbie Palace had asked her to marry him. It was really romantic and he was tickled pink with himself. As soon as Tristan heard about the engagement, he decided to throw an impromptu party to celebrate. Harry had planned to have the evening off and go into Albi that evening to meet up with some of his English friends who were on holiday there. Tristan told him instead to invite them all out to Mas de Lavande instead to join the party. Why?

After the earlier upset, we were persona non grata. Again Tristan didn't say anything to us. It was too difficult to ask him to set aside time for a meeting with us. There was so much going on with the workshop and guests and now a party, it wasn't an appropriate time. Steve and I just carried on with our work and with whatever was needed for the engagement celebrations.

The plan was to seat everyone at dinner on the art studio terrace. This meant pulling out the trestle tables and benches and extra chairs needed to be carried over from the dining room as well as all the glassware, crockery and cutlery. I grabbed the largest tablecloths from the drawers in the house kitchen and overlapped these across all the table-tops. It was the perfect place to have dinner and it would be the first time the studio and terrace would be used as a dining area. Guests could have a drink and mingle in the garden first.

As the afternoon turned to evening, the weather began to look iffy. We were continually looking at the sky.

'Excuse me, Tristan,' I heard Steve say. 'The forecast is for rain and those clouds are looking very heavy. It may be better to set up inside the studio to keep everyone and everything dry.'

'Nonsense! It's going to be absolutely fine,' Tristan swirled, gesticulating wildly at the sky. He wouldn't be persuaded otherwise. Steve and I exchanged glances.

Mountains of cutlery lined the table for all the courses, along with many glasses, side plates and the salads. Steve and I walked around the garden, refilling glasses. As soon as the cooks came out to advise dinner was ready, everyone moved to the tables on the terrace, filled plates and with a drink in hand sat down to eat. It was only a matter of minutes and a few mouthfuls of food before the heavens opened. Down came the rain, fast and furious.

Everyone shot out of their chairs, grabbed their plates and glasses and scrambled to get inside the studio. It was pandemonium. We rushed to clear the tables and to bring them indoors. Of course the tablecloths were sodden. Inside the studio Tristan clapped his hands.

'Annemarie, Steve, we need dry tablecloths and towels to wipe down the tables, thank you.'

Steve and I dashed back to the house for fresh linen and reset the tables. What a ridiculous situation. We scooped up the wet towels and tablecloths and dumped them on the floor beside the back door to the laundry for us to deal with later. We could hear Tristan clapping his hands again, calling for us. We needed to hurry and get dinner back on track.

At last dinner was over, plates cleared and dishwashers loaded. The cook, his wife and their new best friend, Harry, had joined the party. Harry was giving us a wide berth. Guests chatted with Steve and me and with our work day finished, we, too, joined in and had a glass or two of wine. I was a bit uncomfortable after the earlier incident but the other staff were having a lovely time, why couldn't we, too? The young crowd from Albi bowled in late, turned up the music and headed for the drinks table. At a glance I guessed they were well on their way before they even arrived at Mas de Lavande.

I said goodnight to the guests within hearing distance and went off to my bed. A few of the older workshop artists had already drifted off. When I left, the music was blaring and the party was in full swing. It looked to be getting pretty wild. Thank goodness our place was further down the path and away from the noise so I could get some sleep.

The next morning we were up at 6.00 a.m. The artists' workshop day was due to begin at 9.00 a.m. Steve had gone to take care of the animals, tidy up the studio and terrace and set up the pool area. I made my way to the house kitchen, using the French doors at the back of the house. I didn't want to wake anyone by using the back door.

I couldn't believe my eyes. Sleeping bodies lay sprawled on the living room sofas and on the outdoor furniture. Half-empty bottles, glasses and paper napkins were strewn around. Partially eaten food was ground into carpets. Two of the coffee tables were upended on the floor. Ashtrays were overflowing and the place stank of cigarettes and stale booze. I didn't know where to start.

Steve arrived in the kitchen with a tray of dirty glasses from the studio and whispered, 'What the hell's happened here?'

The living areas and the kitchen were an absolute pigsty.

'They must have moved the party down here in the early hours,' I whispered back.

Trying not to wake anyone, we got started. Steve removed bottles and as much rubbish as he could. I cleared plates, unloaded and loaded dishwashers and cleaned up the kitchen. It was a marathon effort. Some of the workshop guests arrived on the scene and were shocked at the state of the living room, not to mention rather weary from lack of sleep due to all the noise during the night. They'd come to Mas de Lavande for the artists' workshop and to enjoy the peace and quiet of the French countryside, the wine and food. Shelley had been the big drawcard for them and an unruly party had certainly not been on their agenda.

We cleared some space so they could at least sit somewhere clean and handed them a very welcome cup of tea or coffee. Breakfast would have to wait. Dishevelled and comatose bodies slept through it all. We managed to get some semblance of order back into the rooms and it was about 10 a.m. when the living room door opened. Tristan stood there with young Harry, gaping at the scene before them. The place was looking much better but there was still plenty to do to put it to rights once everyone woke. Tristan caught our eyes.

'Annemarie, Steve, bring black rubbish bags to the laundry area immediately,' he snarled.

Oh no! I'd gone to bed and had forgotten entirely about all the wet tablecloths and towels. I'd come in a different way that morning, instead of the usual back door, so didn't see them. Smelly, lumpen piles of wet towels and tablecloths sat on the floor in a puddle of water. It looked terrible. Unfortunately the laundry area was a much-used thoroughfare by guests and family alike. I started to apologise but it was no use. Tristan was so angry.

'What on earth is wrong with you people?' he hissed. 'You've been so insulting to young Harry and now you haven't even bothered to bag all these and take them out to the barn. What were you thinking, leaving it all there in the walkway where all the guests could see it?'

It wasn't deliberate on our part; both of us had completely forgotten about them with everything else going on.

Having spent the early morning cleaning up from the party, with still more to be done, as well as looking after the guests, I

162 • MY FRENCH PLATTER

totally lost control of myself. I couldn't help it. There were no civilities from Tristan, no 'thank you for everything you've done this morning and making the guests comfortable'. Nothing. That was the last straw for me. At that moment all the snipes and not-quite-rights and feeling put-upon filled my head.

'What is wrong with *you*?' I spluttered. 'We've been working since 6.00 a.m. to put the place to rights. You took no notice of anyone last night who told you it was about to rain. Nothing we do satisfies you; we can do no right in your eyes. Why is it we get on so well with everyone else who comes to the property, guests and tradespeople alike? But somehow we don't with you?'

If I hadn't felt so upset, I would have laughed at the response of, 'you Antipodeans; you have no idea of class'. We knew who had class and who didn't. Conversely what was being referred to was the British class structure. Somehow, in his mind, we New Zealanders were of a much lower class than his imagined British pedigree. Well, that was an absolute joke. Unfortunately, then and there, it wasn't in the least bit funny. How I wished we were dealing with Richard—a seemingly much more rational and calm person.

From that moment on, there was no longer any semblance of help from Harry. The following morning I arrived in the kitchen to find a note from him. It told me to clean the floors, empty the dishwashers, clean the stovetops and to do the breakfasts. I was furious but ignored it. Who did he think he was? Harry clearly felt supported and could do whatever he pleased. And he certainly did. Harry was poolside all that day.

I poured my heart out to Sarah in a Skype chat later that evening, tears rolling down my face as I told her honestly and openly everything that had gone on.

'Please, Sarah,' I sobbed. 'Can you help us to improve matters with Tristan? I don't know what to do anymore. Can you provide some sort of mediation please? I want to make this right. We're doing, and have done, the best we can. We need to have a proper conversation. I'm sorry but Harry has been hopeless. I don't want to offend you but he's doing the bare minimum.'

Sarah was nodding, fidgeting with things on her desk, not even looking at me.

'OK, OK. Let me talk to Tristan and I'll get back to you,' she said.

Great, I thought. *Something will, at last, be done to resolve issues.* Two days later the first artists' workshop had ended and over the next few days we put the house back to rights. We had five days' breathing space before the next workshop would begin.

Sarah sent an email that night to say she and Richard were coming across from London. They arrived at Mas de Lavande the next day and Sarah came straight down to our cottage. My heart was starting to hammer in my chest. Sarah began. She'd spoken to Tristan and, unbelievably, we were to be off the property by 6 p.m. that day.

From having a home and the use of a car, we had eight hours to pack, find accommodation and a vehicle. Without divulging details there were trumped-up accusations made to engender fear of reprisals for us should we not comply.

We were shocked. I'd thought we would be sitting down and talking, resolving issues on both sides and creating a pathway forward. What a horrible state of affairs. We were 12,000 miles from home, had no family, no car and limited language capabilities. We found ourselves with very few euros and nowhere to go.

Thank heavens for Doug and Siobhan. As soon as I sent them a text to say things had turned very sour and we had to leave by 6 p.m., Siobhan rang. 'Come to us,' she said firmly. 'The bedroom is all ready for you. I thought this might happen.'

Later Doug and Siobhan told us they'd held back divulging what had gone on with the previous guardians. It had been the same scenario: hard-working, got on well with everyone but never enough. One of them had snapped one day, packed their bags and walked out. Doug and Siobhan had hoped that with us there, Tristan would finally be happy.

Steve isn't one to walk away from injustice. Me? I couldn't wait to leave. I was exhausted, stressed and very, very unhappy. Steve was all set to squat.

'They can't do this to us. It's not legal.' He fumed.

'I know you're right but I can't stand it any longer. I'm not interested in squatting just because we're in the right. I've absolutely had it. If you want to stay, you stay. I'm going to Doug and Siobhan's!' I yelled at him.

As we argued back and forth, I pulled clothes from the wardrobe and drawers and threw them into the open suitcases on the bed. Tristan arrived at the cottage in the middle of me packing to add his two penn'orth[1] now that Sarah had delivered the news. I shut the bedroom door on him, leaving Steve to talk to Tristan, and kept on filling the cases. I couldn't bear to look at the man.

There was a knock on the French doors. *Who the hell is it now?* I thought. I opened the bedroom door and saw Tristan had gone and Richard was standing there.

'I wanted to say goodbye,' he said quietly. 'I'm so sorry it ended this way. It didn't need to. I guess you've seen that Tristan can be tricky to deal with,' he added, looking at us sadly.

What an understatement.

'Anyway, all the very best and thank you.'

'It was good of you to come and see us. Thank you, Richard, very much,' I said, still shaking from the news and my argument with Steve. Steve and I shook Richard's hand and he turned and left.

Really at that moment we should have driven off to find a lawyer or gone to the police station. Even if the law was on our side, I certainly had no intention of staying.

The positive out of this situation was that *I* had drawn up the employment agreement. *I* had put in a two-month notice clause which had been agreed to and signed off at the beginning of this debacle. Before we left that fateful day, Steve got it in writing that we would receive payment for these two months and we could have use of the car for a couple of days. Belatedly we were offered two nights' accommodation in a B&B. Too little, too late.

As we headed down the drive, with the car full of hastily packed suitcases and supermarket bags, Tristan decided to make an appearance. He approached Steve's side of the car, calling, 'Bye. Thanks so much for everything.'

Talk about Jekyll and Hyde. So-called other friends of his, who had flown across with Sarah and Richard, stood in the doorway, watching us leave. To have him stand beside the car, saying thanks so much for everything was so bizarre. I wonder how he explained our hasty departure to his 'friends'.

I refused even to acknowledge that he was there and kept my eyes firmly on the driveway. My jaw ached from clenching and gritting my teeth. Steve put his foot down and we accelerated away. Away from all the stress and misery, our first French home and work experience.

Now what?

---

1. Opinions or thoughts.

29

Down, but Certainly not out

To misquote Charles Dickens: it had been the worst of times and the best of times.

The worst of times had been arriving at Mas de Lavande and thinking *I can't do this.* Having to deal with the dilapidated old kitchen, with its crumbling walls and ceiling and filthy ovens was very difficult, as was coping with the old utensils and pots and pans, blunt and chipped knives and cracked crockery. I never envisaged having to spend days cleaning, cleaning, cleaning and washing, washing, washing before we could even begin to start work. Hearing so many negatives about previous property managers' experiences, being harangued for events beyond our control, being shouted at and belittled in front of others were soul-destroying experiences. We were promised so much but nothing was ever delivered. We would wake to endless emails demanding this be done, that be done then situations and words were twisted and misconstrued. It had been difficult to watch Steve pulled from pillar to post. I'd cried more tears in those three months than I'd shed in ten years.

The best of times included the welcome we'd received from the French and English people we'd met. The warm, balmy nights Steve and I sat at our rusty outdoor table, with the sun setting, enjoying a simple dinner, a glass of rosé in hand and the animals around us were perfect.

I loved watching Steve and Gabriel lay the foundations of the kitchen garden, rotary hoe the plots and plant the first of the summer vegetables, with the two of them sitting down together drinking coffee, one practising his French, the other his English. Then there were our fun, relaxing evenings with Doug and Siobhan, just laughing and laughing.

There were so many other pleasurable moments: completing the housework, dinner in the oven, the lamps all lit, cushions plumped and bedrooms looking perfect. Having coffee at our local bakery and Antoinette greeting us with kisses each time, making us feel welcome. Watching the changes in the fields, the wheat ripening, the harvesting, meeting the tractors with hay bales on the narrow roads. The bursting-through of the yellow faces of the sunflowers and driving along country lanes to local markets. Walking up in the early evening light for a glass of wine at the local *tabac* and calling a friendly *bon soir* to the neighbours. The gourmet market night with Gabriel and family and Siobhan and Doug and children. Our days away exploring, plus our music nights in the Sports Bar.

After an ugly, strained day, we arrived at Siobhan and Doug's with all our worldly possessions in the back of the car. They were waiting on the doorstep as we drove in. I fell into Siobhan's open arms, silent tears sliding down my face, only just holding myself together. How we'd met such fabulous, kind people I didn't know. Their door had been open to us since the day we arrived and we felt we'd known them forever. They'd seen first-hand what went on and had experienced others coming and going. They understood exactly what we'd been through. It all made sense then, why we found our cottage in the mess we did. We'd left in a hurry, exactly as others had done.

The following day Siobhan, Doug and the children left for a week away down south. Steve and I were lucky to have the house to ourselves. We could lick our wounds and recover from immense mental and physical tiredness after all the hard work over the previous months, as well as the emotional stress of that last week.

It felt so good to wake that first morning and know we didn't have to crawl out of bed at 6.00 a.m. to start work. It was a day of dozing and replying to the most wonderful, supportive emails from family and friends. Both our sons rang. It was so good to hear their voices at such an awful time. What a funny role reversal it was as they counselled *us* rather than the other way round.

In the following days, we put out feelers to those we'd met to ask if there was any similar work in the area. The response was amazing. An email had gone out via a vast network of connected friends advising that we were available. People asked around for us for work and accommodation. Fabienne, Siobhan's French friend, came over and helped us register on a French employment website.

We decided to take a few days to think about 'where to from here?' We were in frequent touch with Ann and Kevin, other friends at home, my sisters and Gin and Dave, who were now based in London. Andy and Emma, dear friends we'd met years ago when he was seconded to New Zealand, had called from their Dorset holiday home with generous offers to go to either their London or Dorset homes or to join them on holiday in Tuscany. Andy also offered legal advice, if we needed it, a little further down the track. Margo (whom I'd been friends with in New Zealand since our teens) and Tom in Glasgow also offered a place with them, as did my cousin Catherine, who lives in the Cotswolds. Everyone was so kind and offered their support from afar. All we wanted then was to get the basic payout of what was due to us.

Never had such a thing happened to either of us in our lives. We were holding onto the fact that we were honourable, kind, hard-working and ethical people. All we'd done was stand up for ourselves.

There are two sides to every story. I've given you my version and how it affected me. I won't pretend we were perfect, because we bit back.

30

Onwards and Upwards

The weather for the next week was sweltering. We sat behind closed shutters and windows to keep out the intense heat of the day. Boris and Thibault (dog and cat) were splayed out on the tiles, trying to keep their bodies cool. There was talk of temperatures of 40°C or more and it felt like it. Closing the shutters to keep out the heat made the house very dark. We had to turn the lights on but at least the house was at a pleasant temperature.

Six days had passed since we'd arrived at Siobhan and Doug's and Steve and I were back to our old selves again. It was only when I looked back that I realised how bad things had become and how miserable we'd both been as we slogged through the days to get the work done.

During that week we'd returned the car to Mas de Lavande and had one last upsetting encounter with Sarah but finally what was due to us was in the bank. I could breathe again. There was no need to have anything more to do with Mas de Lavande. We were free, free, free!

Even after all the adversity and drama that had gone on, neither of us was ready to return to New Zealand. The experience hadn't put us off and we wanted to continue to live in

France. We loved it. So getting back online to the job market, I answered a few advertisements. After several emails and a long chat on speakerphone, we went down in Siobhan's car to a little village near Castres to meet Mr and Mrs Grainger, who wanted caretakers. Their situation was different from our first employment as they didn't do rentals. They only had friends to stay and a maximum of six at a time. We had to hide our grins while thinking, *Is that all?* That would be a doddle after looking after the number of people we'd had at Mas de Lavande.

Mr and Mrs Grainger were obviously comfortable and the house (one of three they owned around the world) was stunning. The original façade (old stone château with blue shutters) was retained but the interior had been completely gutted and rebuilt. The kitchen was beautiful, straight out of a glossy interiors magazine and looked like a Smallbone of Devizes kitchen. It had been made in the UK and brought across to France and fitted by the makers. Its cabinetry was a lustrous cream colour, topped with dark, highly polished, timber work surfaces. All the appliances were Miele, including an induction hob. The splashback was created from old Italian tiles and depicted a colourful scene of roosters and chickens in a field.

All the bedrooms had an en-suite, and there was also a separate, two-bedroom guest apartment with a small, fitted kitchen. The drawing room, formal lounge and snug were styled with antiques, paintings and French and English plates. The fabrics, trims and tassels were French, Italian and English. I loved it all. It also had a small gymnasium, a pool and a glorious garden. I'm sure I haven't left anything out…

Mr Grainger jokingly referred to our accommodation across the courtyard as the 'servants' quarters'. The two-bedroom, two-bathroom apartment was modern, with a lovely kitchen. A narrow spiral staircase in the centre of the room led up to the bedrooms. How would I get my suitcase up there? It looked to be total luxury after what we'd been living in. The owners were friendly people with obvious good senses of humour. They even looked at us now and again! He poured us lovely wine and Mrs Grainger made delicious roasted salmon and ratatouille for our dinner. We had arrived at 5.30 p.m. and I was shocked to see it was after 11 p.m. by the time we stood up to leave.

Imagine spending such a pleasant evening with prospective employers. The salary offered was double what we'd been getting and the hours were weekdays 8.30 a.m. to 5 p.m., with a little cooking here and there and help of course when their friends arrived. Sounded like an effortless life after the hours we'd been working. The kindness of Mr and Mrs Grainger restored my faith that, really, most people the world over are kind, caring and reasonable.

As we drove home discussing everything then rehashed it again the next morning, something was holding us both back from saying, 'Yes, we really want this one.' It was a fantastic job, no mistaking that. Mr and Mrs Grainger were lovely people and the caretaker accommodation was excellent. We hadn't yet been offered the job but Steve and I went with our gut instinct and left it there. We were both so nervous about making another mistake.

Andy and Emma's incredibly generous offer to stay with their family at a villa in Tuscany was just too hard to resist. With the decision made to stay in France, we needed to buy a car and after investigating flight costs we decided to drive to Tuscany instead. We would put the airfare money into buying a car. We purchased our Renault Megane from a dealer Doug had bought their two vehicles from—someone he trusted.

While still at Mas de Lavande, I'd found and contacted another prospective employer, Mrs Porter, whose holiday home was in Provence. We'd been corresponding for about a month, off and on. Reading between the lines, she sounded a lovely woman. Their current caretakers were retiring after 15 years. I didn't want any secrecy and, as with Mr and Mrs Grainger, I was completely honest with her that we were now available because we'd been asked to leave. Astoundingly she said they were still very happy to meet us. They would help us with petrol money, give us dinner and have us stay the night on our way through to Tuscany. Gosh how generous. They, too, only had family and friends to stay so there would be no paying guests. Steve and I both love Provence so we were keen to explore this option.

Walking out of the door one morning, I heard my laptop ping as an email came in. I'd received a reply to yet another job I'd applied for.

Hello, Annemarie, thank you for your application but I already have a shortlist of people. However, if none of these people proves suitable, would you mind me getting back in touch?

Of course we wouldn't mind. We had nothing else firmed up. Next minute a second email popped up from the same man.

Sorry, I forgot to add the link to the property in my last email. Here you go. Thank you!

Lo and behold, this place was only 20 minutes from Siobhan and Doug's home. It was gorgeous and it did rentals. The location meant we'd still be able to meet up with Siobhan and Doug, Gabriel and Suzanne. Plus we knew the area so well. Perfect. I quickly replied.

Hello again. We're currently very close to your property and know the area well. We meet all your criteria, looking after both guests and property, and can turn our hands to most things. Would you mind taking our application seriously and add us to your shortlist please? We're heading down to

*Tuscany and will be away for a week but would very much
like to be considered.*

Ping! He'd responded.

*No problem. Get in touch when you return from Italy and
we'll make a time. We, too, are having a holiday in Italy.
We look forward to meeting you.*

Fantastic! I was getting excited about our prospects.

We were no longer running around like headless chooks,
working all the hours God sent so I told Steve to stop buying my
daily *pain aux raisin* from the bakery. I wanted to try and keep
off the weight that I'd lost. I had no idea how much that was but
my shorts were falling off my hips and I'd said goodbye to the
'muffin' look. I should have kept quiet. Steve decided then and
there we should go walking to help keep our weight off. He
dragged me and Boris (Siobhan and Doug's massive Rhodesian
Ridgeback dog) outdoors.

Boris leapt up and down in anticipation and bounded off
into the rather dense forest at the end of the lane. I thought we'd
lost him at one point as I searched for ages. He didn't come back
to me when I called and called. Finally I caught up with Steve
on the return journey and Boris was there with him, safe and
sound. In the heat of the morning, Boris was panting like crazy.
Every few metres he would drop to his haunches on the grass
verge, furiously trying to get his breath back. It was so difficult
to try and coax him to his feet to walk a little further. He was
such a lump. I was starting to get very worried about him and
was glad we were very near to home.

Finally we got in the door. Boris' breathing was so laboured
and his tongue was hanging out on the floor. Every now and
then, there was this loud galumphing noise as he drew in a deep
breath and swallowed his saliva, of which there were copious
amounts. I was frightened as he didn't seem to be able to get

enough air. I quickly went online and discovered this was how dogs cool themselves. I was to put a cool, damp towel on him as well as to have plenty of water available.

I leapt about, wet an enormous towel and draped it over Boris as he tried to draw breath. I thought he was going to have a heart attack and die on the kitchen floor.

This dog was the much-loved and cherished pet of the children. The son often lay down with Boris, his arms flung tightly around his neck, giving him lots of kisses. I would have been in serious trouble if darling Boris snuffed it on my watch. I quickly rang Siobhan and Doug and explained the situation. They laughed down the phone at me.

'Annemarie, what on earth did you think you were doing taking the dog out for a walk? He *never* goes for a walk; it's been a huge shock to his system. Don't worry, we're sure he'll come right. It's happened before,' Doug laughed. After about an hour, Boris eventually settled and fell straight asleep, exhausted. I'd had frightening visions of having to give dear Boris mouth-to-mouth to resuscitate him.

31

We are so Lucky

During the week we had to ourselves, we invited Doug Snr to come for dinner. He brought a friend from his village with him, Suzee, who turned out to be a fabulous little gem and very kindly emailed yet more people about our job needs. As a result of all this emailing, we secured not one but two interim jobs.

The first was a few months' work with a US interior designer who had a holiday home not far from Toulouse and needed help with her property and guests. We would start there as soon as we returned from Italy. She's a very private person so for confidential reasons I'm unable to tell you about our time there but what a beautiful property she had.

At the second job, we would have a two-bedroom cottage in exchange for 30 hours' work a week on the property. We were thrilled. The cottage had its own swimming pool—even better.

Steve and I drove to Lisle-sur-Tarn to meet the owners, Denise and Ian, and to take a look at what needed doing. The work primarily consisted of taming a very overgrown, formal garden. We had no idea how long we would be there; it might be two weeks or two months. All we knew was that we couldn't go too long without an income and Denise and Ian had a family that would be renting the cottage from the beginning of December. We would need to have a permanent job before then.

With a sense of excitement, light hearts and the worry of our immediate future sorted, Steve and I packed up the car and started our journey through to Tuscany. Our first stop was the small town of Entrecasteaux in Provence.

Here we met another set of prospective employers, Mr and Mrs Porter. Again a beautiful home with a mixture of English and French furnishings but this time much more French country than the last. The house had lots of colourful pottery and was furnished in a relaxed, classic style. It was very cute. Mrs Porter was very warm and welcoming. Mr Porter was a little aloof but pleasant enough. He came through the door, greeted us in French and immediately turned to Steve and chatted on in French, testing Steve's comprehension of what he was saying. Luckily Steve understood and replied in French. Test one passed! We got down to business and went through the job description together. We also had time with the current caretakers so we could get a thorough overview of the job.

'Annemarie and Steve, since we emailed, friends have arrived from the UK. We're having a dinner party tonight. Please don't think me rude but would you mind awfully having dinner in the village tonight? Our treat, of course,' Mrs Porter said graciously.

'Of course we don't mind. We understand totally. Please, it's very kind of you to offer but we can do this for ourselves,' I replied, feeling a bit embarrassed.

'No, no, I insist. This is our treat. You've deviated from your holiday to come for this interview so we would like to pay. And please, make sure you give me your fuel and toll receipts in the morning. We'll reimburse you for those, too,' she said.

'Well, thank you so much, Mrs Porter. You've been more than kind; you've been incredibly generous. Thank you again,' I said.

Our bedroom for the night was in a self-contained cottage which overlooked the pool. It had pale lemon walls with a pretty blue toile fabric bed cover and there was a fully tiled en-suite. The downstairs kitchen was a great size with everything to hand we could possibly want. This was where their cook, whom they brought with them from the UK, would prepare poolside dinners. This attractive cottage was used for friends and family when there was an overflow in the house.

After a refreshing dip in the pool and a quick change into clean clothes, we drove back down the long, narrow drive to the village to find their highly recommended restaurant.

It was yet another balmy evening and lots of locals and tourists were enjoying dinner outdoors. People sat with a glass of wine at a bar or strolled around the town arm in arm, chatting. Music filtered out from the many restaurants and cafés. After we'd ordered, we, too, sat back at our outdoor table with a delicious glass of Provencal wine. Both of us enjoyed just watching others around us while waiting for our dinner.

'Do you know,' I said leaning across the table towards Steve, 'I could get very used to this life—being on the other side.' He just grinned at me.

We talked and talked during our dinner about this particular house and this job.

'I can't believe they offered us three times what we were getting at Mas de Lavande, can you, hon?' asked Steve. 'That's so generous.'

'I know it is but they want us for at least two years and to be honest, I don't think I could cope with living in that cottage over the winter. It's just too gloomy, dark and it's rather small,' I responded.

'We don't have to decide tonight. Let's just think about it while we're in Italy. Anyway they haven't even offered us the job yet,' Steve said.

In the meantime Mr and Mrs Grainger, whom we went to see in Castres, had emailed saying they would like to offer us the job. We were so flattered but politely declined.

'I felt a bit awful saying "no thank you" to Mr and Mrs

Grainger, Steve, but I didn't want to commit to two years in Castres either. I know we would have made friends over time but I really like the area we're living in now,' I told him.

'Me too. We've got to know it pretty well. Also we've got a couple of friends there already. Meeting new people isn't easy,' he agreed. 'Anyway did you notice how Mr Grainger referred to our accommodation as "the saaarvants' quarters" in that exaggerated way?' Steve asked. 'I know he said it jokingly but I'd hate for him to adopt that frame of mind with us as time went on. See us as servants, rather than employees. D'you know what I mean?'

I knew exactly what he meant. Both of us were very nervous about making another mistake with the people we chose to work for.

'I know it sounds like we're being very picky but gut instinct is a good indicator to go with and mine said "no",' I told Steve, moving the wine glasses as our main course arrived.

'Agreed!' Steve stated. 'This confit of duck looks delicious. Let's forget about it all and just enjoy our dinner and a night out. Bon appetit,' he said, raising his wine glass.

Mid-morning the next day, we met up with Mr and Mrs Porter for coffee.

'It's been a pleasure to meet you both,' Mrs Porter smiled at us. 'Now here's the reimbursement of your fuel and toll costs and dinner last night. Did you enjoy the food? Isn't it a sweet little place? We often go. The staff are wonderful, too,' she enthused, handing us a wad of notes.

'It was just great, thank you both,' Steve said. 'You've been extremely generous to us. It's been very nice to meet you too. Thank you for the opportunity. We'd better get on our way. We have a long drive ahead of us.'

'Mr Porter and I have one more couple to interview. We'll let you know by next weekend where the job stands. In the meantime you have a good talk and a think whether this job will work for you both. Have a super time in Tuscany. It's one of my favourite places to visit,' Mrs Porter said, opening the front door.

32

Tuscany

The house we stayed in in Tuscany, La Civettaia in Ghizzano, was just beautiful. Hilly and her husband, Christiano, ran the villa for their employers. They were warm, fun people. Andy, Emma and family had been delayed in London by a storm so Steve and I were the first to arrive. Hilly took us on a tour of the house. Every bedroom was so elegantly furnished. Ours had a super king bed with an upholstered headboard and a large, two-seater wicker sofa. Through a door to one side of the bed was a separate dressing room with a built-in wardrobe and chest of drawers. On the other side, another door opened into our bathroom, which was almost as big as the bedroom. The floor was muted terracotta tiles, as was the recessed open shower. A twin hand basin vanity ran the full length of one wall and a very deep bath sat in the middle of the room. No expense had been spared to make the villa a comfortable place to stay. The dining room roof was a vaulted ceiling and a hand-painted mural in aqua, terracotta and soft greens depicting an olive grove scene covered one entire wall. It was exquisite.

Hilly and Christiano were so welcoming. As there were only the two of us, we insisted they had a drink and dinner with us, which we helped prepare.

We knew what it was like to be on their side of the bench. They both said they found it very unusual but so nice to be having drinks and dinner with the guests. Steve and I made the excuse that we needed fresh conversation as we'd been cooped up in the car together for six hours on each of the last two days.

Just as we were putting the last of the dinner dishes away, Andy, Emma, the family and a couple of the kids' friends came through the door. It had been a long day of travel for them. They'd eaten at the airport but Andy was keen for a glass of wine and to sit outdoors to chat, catch up and enjoy the night sky. Andy and Emma rented a house somewhere special each year and they both agreed that this had to be the best place so far. We sat up late into the night and watched the sky blacken. What a spectacular show of fork lightning that night, flashing across the rolling landscape, with great claps of thunder overhead. Torrential rain followed and continued for much of the night. This would have been a relief for the locals and the parched earth alike.

Andy and Steve took the boys to play golf next day. Emma, her friend Elaine (who was also staying) and I took ourselves up the road to explore the little village of Ghizzano. We left the luscious 20-something-year-olds back at the house, lying around the pool, pursuing a Mediterranean tan. The café we chose had a set-up the same as that at our old *tabac* back in France. One side sold the meats, cheeses and necessities of life; the other, coffee, alcohol and gelato. The difference was that in Ghizzano, there were a lot of girlie calendars lining the walls, one dating back to 2007. Signor must have been particularly fond of the girl on the front of this calendar to have kept her so long.

One morning before breakfast and while the rest of the household slept, Steve and I slipped out of the house and hiked up to the house ruin sitting on the hill across from us. At the crazy hour of 7 a.m., the air was fresh, cool and clear. Our only companions were the birds flitting about and singing above us. The views were breathtaking. Some of the estates we could see were immense, with substantial old homes. All were surrounded by the signature Mediterranean cypress trees, lining the driveways and the rolling brown hills. It had been a long, dry summer.

Our time in Tuscany was a luxurious, relaxing and fabulous break after all our drama. We managed to get to San Gimignano, Lucca, Volterra and Certaldo. Steve was very keen to get his photo taken, holding up the Leaning Tower of Pisa, citing that he couldn't come all this way and not do it. What a tourist. Andy, Emma and I went to Certaldo that day, which was a lovely little town. The three of us caught the funicular up the slope to the old part of town to have a look around. We ate our salad lunch outside on the street, enjoying a glass of Prosecco with it. As a memento of our wonderful week away, Emma and I couldn't resist purchasing a pretty, painted Italian ceramic pot each. I smile to myself every time I look at it on my shelf at home.

In the Collegiate Church of Santa Maria Assunta in San Gimignano, we saw the beautiful ochre and deep blue colours of the detailed frescoes. We climbed to a great lookout point which offered a tremendous view out over the surrounding landscape. Next was Volterra which has an excavated Roman theatre and the remains of an ancient acropolis which had been turned into a park area. Volterra is known for its alabaster and some of the carvings were so delicately detailed. Lastly we headed to Lucca, which is a very beautiful walled city with fabulous shopping and architecture. Hiring bikes in Lucca is a great way to get around and see everything but the cyclists can be a bit tricky for pedestrians at times.

What a wonderful and generous treat, sharing a special week with our friends. When not touring we spent our time reading, swimming, eating fabulous food and drinking rich, ruby-red Italian wine. Most evenings we spent many hours at the dinner table but also playing music, cards or Scrabble. Andy and Emma did think I was trying to hoodwink them when I said, yes, you can have XI and XU in Scrabble.

Steve was thrilled to get in some golf as he hadn't played since he left New Zealand. It was great fun to have all the young ones with us, too, for the week. They provided terrific entertainment, with a lot of coercing/banter from Andy. He had us all playing a game called Matthew, Mark, Luke and John one night after dinner. We'd never heard of it and it was both challenging and fun trying to keep the mind concentrated after a couple of wines. Another afternoon the girls had Emma and me up dancing with the rest of the young ones, singing the chorus of some latest hit song while they videoed us. It was most certainly a holiday to remember.

33

Tuscany to Toulon

As we left Tuscany, it was as if someone had said, 'Shut the door; summer's over. Pull on your sweater and jeans.' As we drove to Toulon in France, the temperature didn't get above 16°C and there was a chilly wind. It felt freezing after the 30°C temperatures we'd been enjoying. When we stopped at one of the Autostrade[1] snack bars, everyone was rugged up in their trousers, jackets and scarves. Alas, not us. I didn't have a stitch of warm clothing with me. I'd been holidaying in Tuscany. Why would I need anything? The rain had set in, too, making it a miserable, bleak day.

My terrible fears and stress while driving on the Italian motorways weren't as bad then as they had been during our month-long trip in 2008. The speed of the cars and the width of the roads were now less of a problem for me. Still, there were a few heated discussions about how 'one' drove, followed up with how 'one' should be quiet. If 'one' couldn't be quiet, then 'get behind the wheel and do it oneself'. How rude. Surprisingly Steve and I were still talking to each other when we arrived in Toulon—just. There would be an endurance test a few days later, with the two of us side by side in the car for the rest of the journey back to Doug and Siobhan's.

Steve and I got soaked as we left the car park beside the Toulon train station. We needed to get to the tourist office to find a B&B and quickly. It was getting late and we had nowhere to sleep.

Steve finally managed to find us a place to stay, via the phone, after several attempts. Of course it would *have* to be set within a maze of tiny streets in the old part of Toulon which would need careful negotiating. At least it had a garage and we could stow the car safely overnight.

Our room was very cute, with the bed set up on the mezzanine floor, accessed by a very narrow and steep flight of stairs. It was quite bizarre as a large bath with a hand-held shower and a hand basin were set in one corner of the living area. The space surrounding the bath and basin was beautifully tiled in a Provençal style but with no curtain to pull, water splashed all over the floor. We endeavoured to limit the damage by laying a towel on the floor to soak up any spills. Our hosts were very welcoming. She didn't speak English and I didn't speak French but, somehow, we got along just fine, as most women do all over the world, regardless of language barriers.

An email came in from Mrs Porter, just as we were going out of the door to dinner.

Hello, Annemarie and Steve. I do hope you had the most wonderful time in Tuscany. Mr Porter and I have made the decision that we think you are the people we would like to have working for us. We would like to offer you the position of guardians for our Provence home and hope you will accept. If you could please let us know your decision in the next couple of days, that would be most appreciated. We very much look forward to working with you.

Steve read the email over my shoulder. 'I'm starving,' he declared. 'Let's talk about this at dinner,' he suggested, grabbing his jacket and the umbrella at the door.

We walked down the hill to our host-recommended restaurant, five minutes from our door and on the waterfront.

Still it was raining and we had to move tables as Steve was getting dripped on from a leak. The owner popped out every ten minutes to lift the 'roof' of the outdoor area with a broom to release the accumulated water down onto the road. Our dinner was beautiful. Steve and I shared foie gras which he followed up with a mixture of prawns, mussels and fish—a poor man's bouillabaisse. Mine was a very nice fish of the day (I have no idea of the name of it), pan-fried with some rice and a few vegetables.

'Decision time then, Steve,' I declared, laying my knife and fork down on my plate. 'Mine is a "no" for the Provence job as well. For all the reasons we talked about when we were at dinner that night. You?'

'I liked the property and I liked the Porters. He was a bit stiff but I'm sure he would have thawed as time went on. Regardless, I agree that our accommodation would have been very dark in winter and it was small. It's a "no" from me too,' he agreed, forking up another mouthful. 'Let's email them before we go to bed. It's done then and the Porters will know where they stand.'

Both of us were yawning. Our 5 a.m. start and a full day of driving had begun to take its toll and bed was beckoning. It was a slow climb back up the path to our hosts.

We composed a quick but polite and thankful email back to Mrs Porter to decline the position. I hoped she wasn't cross with us or thought we'd wasted her time. I couldn't be worrying about it. Our decision was made.

With clear morning skies the next day, we took a long walk along the sea wall of Toulon. We wended our way through little streets and craned our necks to look at the architecture on our path back to a delicious breakfast.

Before leaving Toulon we did a little exploring. Our coffee was with the many cultures in the morning market where we purchased some delicious nibbles to take to Rebecca's. Steve then drove us to the top of Mont Faron, which is the highest point in Toulon. We had incredible views out over the city and the ocean beyond. The road up was so narrow and only had a tiny stone wall to grab us should our wheels veer too close to the edge. I kept looking upwards. It was far too scary to look down or out to the view until we reached the top.

As planned, we stopped at Rebecca's home in Saint-Laurent-d'Aigouze, near Montpellier. We were so looking forward to seeing Rebecca and filling her in on all that had happened since she was with us. Also staying several nights was our friend Ginny from Auckland, who was now living in London. Rebecca went to collect her from the airport while we enjoyed a quiet hour, wandering the garden and reading, awaiting their return.

Checking my watch, I saw it was time to put out the cheeses, olives and meats we'd bought in Toulon. The beers were cold and the rosé had chilled down nicely. As Rebecca pulled up outside the house, Steve and I crossed the lawn to meet them.

---

1. Roads forming the Italian motorway system.

34

We are Delighted to Announce...

It was great to see Ginny and share the minutiae of our lives in a leisurely fashion. We enjoyed a day in Montpellier, wandering the streets and treating ourselves to a good restaurant lunch. Our front-row seats, right on the square, gave us the best people-watching position. With her amazing culinary skills, Rebecca produced delicious dinners and breakfasts for us, eaten in the garden. She did it all with such style and grace. All the old family crockery and silverware came out, with pretty linen napkins on the side. These details added to the pleasure of good food and company.

Steve and I arrived back at Doug and Siobhan's with, surprisingly, no shouting in the car. There was only one near miss—a pedestrian on a pedestrian crossing who jumped out of the way, thank heavens. Steve hadn't even seen her. To give him his due, she was 'lost' within the framework of the car and I knew exactly what he meant.

While we were in Tuscany, we'd received a very excited text message from Doug. He asked us to call him straight away as he had the perfect full-time job for us. Of course we were very curious and rang him. The job would be working for an English couple from London who owned a French holiday home near the town of Gaillac. Currently, they were living and working in New York. They were Mary and Symon, with two adult children.

Our only communication had been a long phone call. The conversation had flowed easily between Mary and me and after a bit of chit-chat, we got down to the serious stuff.

'So where were you working, Annemarie, before your holiday?' asked Mary.

Here we go, I thought. 'Um, we were working for a London couple over the other side of Gaillac, near Brens. Well, we barely got to meet one of the partnership so it really was just one man we dealt with,' I replied.

'Oh, not far from us at all. Who was it you were working for?'

'Well, um, this is where it gets tricky, Mary,' I faltered. 'We had difficulties at the end and under end-of-contract clauses, we're not allowed to say anything.'

'Really? That's intense. Ooh, now I'm intrigued,' she said.

'There's something you need to know,' I blurted. 'I don't want any secrets. We were asked to leave.' The words tumbled out. 'It was all pretty horrible and upsetting actually. Of course there are two sides to every story. But we weren't the first to leave there in a hurry and—'

'Wait a minute!' Mary interrupted. 'I think I know who you're talking about. If it's who I think it is, we've heard a few stories about that place and they're not flattering. The owners are something to do with art, aren't they? I can't remember exactly what, or their names,' she said. 'A few people around here go to the annual art auction at the house. We've never been.'

Goodness, she'd got it in one!

I'm sure she could hear the grin in my voice when I replied, 'I couldn't possibly confirm or deny, Mary!'

Mary wasn't at all fazed by the fact that we'd been asked to leave. She carried on talking about the job and what they needed from guardians at the property. At the end of our chat, Mary suggested, 'Go with Doug and view Combe de Merigot. See what you think. Then we'll have a Skype meeting with Symon and Steve and talk everything through, if you like what you see.'

I was excited as Mary sounded a warm and caring person. This was very important to me.

Steve and I met Doug and Siobhan in the Leclerc car park in Gaillac and tailed them around the edge of town and up the hill. Grapevines climbed up on our left with rolling hills and a few grazing sheep on our right. Halfway up the hill, Doug turned his indicator on to make a right turn. From behind him all we could see were some rather imposing gates and pillars with urns sitting on top. As we reached the same spot and followed them through the gates, it was a 'wow' moment. We couldn't believe our eyes.

'Oh my god, Steve, look at that!' I exclaimed, straining forward in my seat. This was no farmhouse. It was one of the most beautiful French homes I'd ever seen. The style was a classical, 18th-century *domaine,* with a double balustrade staircase leading to the front door. It had a *pigeonnier* tower and sat so perfectly in the landscape. It was a proper estate!

'Incredible,' was all Steve could muster, exhaling loudly. He was also a little in awe of the property. The tree-lined drive wended its way down a gentle slope, crossed a small bridge and turned up a half-circle in front of the house. We came to a stop at the entrance to the great barn, across the drive from the house.

Getting out we just stood for a moment, taking it all in. On one side of the drive there was a huge pond with a little jetty and we could hear and see the breeze whispering through the leafy weeping willow trees lining it.

Doug stood beside his car, hands on hips, grinning at our astonishment.

'Wow! Have you spotted the marble-edged pool?' I exclaimed to Steve.

'Where?' he asked, spinning on the spot.

'Through that ornate wrought-iron gate. What an amazing

covered dining area at the end, too.' I was so impressed, looking at everything.

'There's a kitchenette tucked in behind the dining room,' Doug pointed out, 'and off to the right are changing rooms, a bathroom, an outdoor shower and an undercover area for lounging in, out of the sun.'

'It all looks so elegant. I just love it,' I gushed.

The pool complex was surrounded by a high brick wall, creating a wonderful micro-climate inside. Roses were climbing up trellises, fitted at precise intervals along the walls.

We spent an hour wandering around the house exterior and the immediate grounds, peering in the windows where we could. I knew instantly that we'd 'arrived' and this was exactly where I wanted to live and work. The views were breathtaking. At the rear of the house, a large vineyard climbed up the slope, leading towards the forested ridge. This forest surrounded the back perimeter of the property. What furnishings we could see through the windows were classic French and English. I knew I would be happy working there. I've always loved interiors. When I finally got my own room in my mid-teens, I borrowed books on room design and home management from the local library. Since then I've pored over interior magazines and over the years I've endeavoured to recreate rooms that give an ambience and in a classic style.

The house and property were absolutely beautiful. The guardians' cottage (our place) appeared modern and a decent size. All we could see at the time was the large laundry and a new kitchen, plus a few steps up to the sitting room. We knew that upstairs there were two bedrooms and an en-suite and a bathroom downstairs. As well as the house and the grounds, part of the job would be to take care of two small dogs: a cocker spaniel and a Scottish terrier. They looked adorable in the photo Mary had emailed to us. They had lovely natures, apparently, needed minimal exercise and were good company. I would enjoy having them around. I'd let Steve do any poop-scooping required. There was a backup person if we wanted to go away for a few days, or if we chose to we could take the dogs with us.

After investigating three different permanent jobs, we chose to work for Mary and Symon at Combe de Merigot. The house was about four kilometres from the town of Gaillac. This time everything felt so right. Gaillac was a short drive from our original job and where we already did our household shopping. It was also close to the few friends we'd made in the area, only 45 minutes from Toulouse and 20 minutes from Albi via the motorway. Gaillac had a movie theatre as well as plenty of restaurants, wineries, boutiques, galleries, banks and cafés and a large Friday market—everything we needed in one place.

The warmth and friendliness of the phone call with Mary and seeing the property gave me the feeling that Combe de Merigot was going to be perfect for us. Our joint Skype conversations with Mary and Symon confirmed this as the four of us connected very well. The best thing was that there was no agent or middle man. We would deal directly with them, on everything. They, too, had had some difficulties and hadn't been looking for guardians. Doug had done a lot of work at their home and had an excellent rapport with Mary and Symon. He recommended us to them and them to us and *voilà*!

Once our two interim jobs were completed Steve and I would begin a new chapter in our lives. Both of us were very excited and couldn't wait to get started; this time, with fingers crossed, living the life and working in the sort of job I'd intended for us when I first answered that Gum Tree advertisement.

My French platter was about to be replenished—this time with a lot more delicious French morsels than we'd tasted so far.

You can follow our journey in the sequel, *My French Platter Replenished*, which will be published in 2021.

Message from the Author

I sincerely thank you for reading this book and I hope you enjoyed it. I would be extremely grateful if you could leave a review on Amazon. The following recipes and others can be found on my website. I'd also love to hear your comments and am happy to answer any questions you may have so do please get in touch with me through:

Email: annemarierawson@gmail.com
Facebook: www.facebook.com/annemarie.rawson.1
Website: www.annemarierawson.com
Instagram: www.instagram.com/lateliteadventures

If you enjoy reading memoirs, I recommend you pop over to Facebook group We Love Memoirs to chat with other authors and me.

RECIPES

Grated Raw Beetroot and Carrot Salad

Ingredients

350 g/12 oz carrots, peeled and trimmed
350 g/12 oz raw beetroot, peeled and trimmed
2 shallots, peeled and finely chopped. I use chopped spring onion tops.
2 tsp cumin seeds
2 tbsp olive oil
1 tbsp sherry or red wine vinegar
1 small bunch flat parsley, roughly chopped
Crumbled feta cheese, if you like it

Method

Coarsely grate peeled and trimmed carrots and beetroot, or use a food processor fitted with a grating plate. Put grated carrots and beetroot into a bowl, adding the peeled and finely chopped shallots or spring onion tops.
Dry fry cumin seeds in a small pan until they are hot and pungent. Do not burn. Remove from heat and scatter over vegetables.
Add the olive oil, vinegar and parsley, then toss well. Leave to

marinate for at least 15 minutes before serving. Top with feta cheese, if you like it.

Walnut Meringue with Lemon Curd and Berry Coulis

Ingredients

Meringue
5 large egg whites
300 gm (10 oz) caster sugar
180 gm (6 oz) walnuts, crushed

Lemon curd
3 eggs
250 gm (8.5 oz) caster sugar
Grated rind and juice of 2 large lemons (Lisbon, if possible)
125 gm (4.5 oz) unsalted butter

Coulis
500g (1 lb) strawberries or raspberries
1 tbsp redcurrant jelly
Icing sugar

To serve
300 ml (10 fl oz) cream, whipped
Icing sugar for dredging

Method

Meringue
Line two 20 cm (8 in) sandwich tins with silicone paper or draw two 23 cm (9 in) circles on silicone paper.

Beat egg whites, adding half the sugar as you go, then fold in the remainder at the end of whisking. Mixture should stand up in peaks.

Fold in crushed walnuts with a slotted spoon. Spoon this mixture equally into two tins or onto the silicone paper circles. Bake at 175°C (350°F) for 35-45 minutes, or longer, depending on your oven. Cakes should be crisp on outside. Check after 35 minutes. Turn out carefully onto wire tray when done.

Lemon curd
Beat eggs and sugar with grated lemon rind and juice. Add butter in small pieces. Thicken in heatproof bowl over hot water.

Strawberry (or raspberry) coulis
Puree fruit in liquidiser or food processor. Add redcurrant jelly then icing sugar to taste then sieve.

To assemble
Sandwich the two meringues together with whipped cream and lemon curd.

Dust liberally with icing sugar and serve strawberry (or raspberry) coulis separately.

Note: The lemon curd is also delicious with cream between sponge cakes or as a topping for a pavlova, and is perfect on toast.

Sweet Cherry Pie

Ingredients

900 g (2 lb) pitted or 1 kg (2.2 lb) unpitted fresh cherries
4 tbsp cornflour[1]
135-150 g (4.5-5 oz) sugar (adjust this according to the
sweetness of your cherries)
$\frac{1}{8}$ tsp salt
Juice of half a lemon
¼ tsp almond extract
375 g/13 oz packet of sweet pastry
1 tbsp cold unsalted butter, cut into small pieces
1 egg, beaten with 2 tbsp water
Coarse sugar for decoration

Method

Preheat oven to 200°C (400°F).
Pit the cherries and stir with the cornflour, sugar, salt, lemon and
almond extract gently together in a large bowl.
Roll out half of the chilled dough on a floured work surface to
make 33 cm (13 in) round. Gently place it in a 23 cm (9 in) pie
pan, either by rolling it around the rolling pin and unrolling it

over the pan or by folding it into quarters and unfolding it in the pan. Trim edges to a 1 cm (½ in) overhang.

Spoon filling into pie crust, discarding the majority of the liquid that has pooled in the bowl. Dot the filling with the cold butter. Roll out the remaining dough into a 30 cm (12 in) round on a lightly floured surface, drape it over the filling and trim it, leaving a 2.5 cm (1 in) overhang. Fold the overhang under the bottom crust, pressing the edge to seal it, and crimp the edge decoratively. Brush the egg wash over pie crust then sprinkle with coarse sugar.

Cut slits in the crust with a sharp knife, forming steam vents, and bake the pie in the middle of the oven for 25 minutes. Reduce the temperature to 175°C (350°F). Bake the pie for 25 to 30 minutes more or until the crust is golden. Let the pie cool on a rack.

---

1. US cornstarch.

Chocolate Terrine

Ingredients
75 g (2.5 oz) dark chocolate, melted
7 egg yolks
125 g (4.5 oz) caster sugar
Scant tsp instant coffee dissolved in 2 tbsp hot water
50 g (scant 2 oz) clear honey
140 g (scant 5 oz) unsalted butter, softened
85 g (3 oz) cocoa powder
225 ml (8 fl oz) double cream, whipped
Dash of Cognac

Method
Butter a loaf tin and line with cling film.
Mix together, one by one, the egg yolks, caster sugar, coffee mixture and clear honey into the melted chocolate.
Mix softened butter with cocoa powder then add to the first mixture.
Next fold in the whipped cream, ⅓ at a time, and add the Cognac.
Pour into the loaf tin, fold the cling film over firmly and neatly, then freeze.

Serve straight from the freezer with a warm knife to slice through evenly.
Bon appetit!

Acknowledgements

A huge thank you to all my family and friends who supported us with our move to France, helping me through the rough times and enjoying the great times with us—you know who you are. Also, thank you to those who encouraged the writing of our story once we'd returned to New Zealand.

To Jacky Donovan for her patience and editing prowess in getting this book into shape, ready for publication.

Printed in Dunstable, United Kingdom